C.H. Spurgeon

THE PEOPLE'S PREACHER

Dedication

To my parents, Pam and John, with love and appreciation

C.H. Spurgeon

THE PEOPLE'S PREACHER

PETER MORDEN

Foreword by David Coffey

CWR

Published 2009 by CWR, Waverley Abbey House, Waverley Lane, Farnham, Surrey GU9 8EP, UK. Registered Charity No. 294387. Registered Limited Company No. 1990308.

For list of National Distributors visit our website www.cwr.org.uk

Unless otherwise indicated, all Scripture references are from the Holy Bible: New International Version (NIV), copyright © 1973, 1978, 1984 by the International Bible Society.

Other version used: AV: the Authorised Version

Concept development, editing, design and production by CWR

Cover image and internal images all taken and used with permission of Spurgeons College.

The images on pages 140 and 145 are courtesy of Spurgeons (Spurgeon's Childcare).

Also featured are pictures taken on the set of the film *C.H. Spurgeon – The People's Preacher* (CTA), by:
Lizzie Everard, pages 6, 64 (top 2), 80 (top), 92 (bottom), 118, 134, 150, 164
Andreas Lehmann, pages 14 (both), 26, 36, 50 (both), 80 (bottom), 104
Malcolm Turner, pages 64 (bottom), 92 (top).

Photograph of St Andrew's Street Baptist Church (p38) taken by Judy Morris
Photograph of Menton today (p156) taken by Berthold Werner.
Photograph of author on back cover taken by Dave Lock.

Printed in China by 1010 Printing International Ltd.

ISBN: 978-1-85345-497-4

Contents

Foreword

TRANSLATE the ministry of Charles Haddon Spurgeon into our 21st-century culture and you have a local church pastor with some epic achievements.

When Spurgeon was just twenty-two years of age thousands of Londoners were flocking to hear him preach. For sixty years his sermons were published weekly. By his death 50 million copies had been sold. His sermons were published in forty languages including Arabic, Bengali and Chinese. He was a global influence before the internet age.

And this influence continues. Google the name of C.H. Spurgeon and you will discover hundreds of websites where you can obtain information on his ministry and download his sermons. If you want to understand the enduring influence of this Victorian preacher, visit www.spurgeon.org and read his sermon 'Compel them to come in' based on Luke 14:23. This sermon is reckoned to be one of his most spiritually fruitful sermons in leading people to faith in Christ. Get behind the unfamiliar language and expansive oratory of this 'prince of preachers' and feel the heartbeat of spiritual zeal which thunders through the sermon. I confess when I read a sermon of Spurgeon I want to get up and preach!

This inspiring and illuminating biography by Peter Morden tells the story of Spurgeon's achievements beyond the pulpit, through his social ministries and his concern for the training of pastors, with his lasting legacy of 'Spurgeons' (formerly Spurgeon's Child Care) and Spurgeons Theological College.

The need of the hour remains for there to be wisdom in the pulpit and compassion in the public square. Spurgeon serves as an outstanding mentor to preachers who want to set God's truth on fire and to all who desire to be salt and light Christians making a difference in God's world.

David Coffey,
President of the Baptist World Alliance, Governor of Spurgeons College

Introduction

ON SUNDAY 28 July 1878, Charles Haddon Spurgeon preached in the open air at Rothesay, on the Isle of Bute, in the Firth of Clyde, Scotland. The announcement that Spurgeon would be speaking on the island had been made a few days earlier. The news had quickly spread, by word of mouth and through the local papers, and Spurgeon's visit created much excitement. Many caught one of the steamers that worked the Firth of Clyde, travelling 'doon the watter' from nearby Glasgow in order to hear him. These joined the holidaymakers who were already packing into Rothesay, a Victorian seaside resort particularly popular with the working classes.

When the time came for the service to begin, it was clear that a staggeringly large crowd had gathered. No one is sure exactly how large, but there were perhaps as many as 20,000 people. And they were not disappointed, for when Spurgeon preached he did so with what one observer described as 'marvellous power'. It was a telling description for two reasons. Firstly, and amazingly, everyone in the vast crowd seemed to be able to hear him – and this in the days before microphones and PA equipment! Secondly, thousands of those gathered sensed that God was speaking directly to them through the preacher. Here was 'marvellous power' indeed. Many were so moved that they later perched along the harbour wall in their thousands, waving goodbye to Spurgeon as the boat which was carrying him made its way out of the bay.

Spurgeon the preacher

It is hard for us to imagine a preacher causing such a sensation now, at least in the western world. Of course, Victorian Britain was very different to Britain today. It was an age where popular preachers could and did draw large crowds. But, even for the time, Spurgeon's impact was nothing short of remarkable. If truth be told, nothing like the Rothesay service had really been seen since George Whitefield, the famous eighteenth-century evangelist.

LEFT
Rothesay Bay

And Rothesay was not a one-off; for eager, jostling crowds flocked to hear Spurgeon wherever he went. What's more, he wasn't just an itinerant, a preacher who toured the country taking special services, perhaps repeating the same message wherever he went. No, Spurgeon was first and foremost a local church pastor, able to gather a vast congregation of church members and regular attenders. These people returned week after week, hungry for more of his great preaching. Once again the statistics are hard to believe but, unlike the figure for the Rothesay crowd, they are not estimates. During Spurgeon's ministry 14,693 men and women became members of his London church, nearly 11,000 of these through baptism. At the time of his death the total membership stood at 5,328. The church building could seat just under 6,000 and, Sunday by Sunday, it was usually full. This wasn't just the largest church in Britain. At the time it was the largest in the world

... a tale of large crowds, full buildings and amazing, eloquent, preaching

... but more than a preacher

This is how Spurgeon's story has often been told – a tale of large crowds, full buildings and amazing, eloquent preaching. It's easy to see why people like to concentrate on this area of his life and ministry. The story of Spurgeon the successful preacher is not only exciting and uplifting, it also speaks to us about the importance of having lively, biblical preaching today. This is something I am passionate about, and I have greatly enjoyed writing about this vital aspect of Spurgeon's work. This book, then, tells the story of how Spurgeon spoke words of comfort and strength to countless men and women desperate for help and hope. It is the story of C.H. Spurgeon, the people's preacher.

But, wonderful as this story is, I have wanted to do more in this book than just talk about Spurgeon's preaching. Firstly, I have wanted to look more *broadly*, for Spurgeon wasn't just a preacher. He founded an orphanage and built houses for the poor. In fact, in an age before the welfare state was even thought of, he was involved in an extraordinarily wide range of Christian social activity. He also established a college to train pastors and a society which distributed Christian literature. He was involved in planting over one hundred churches, many of which continue to survive – and thrive – today. And he wrote enough books to make up a small library. Some of these features of his ministry are not often covered, at least not in detail. By looking at them here, hopefully a more rounded picture of Spurgeon emerges.

Secondly, I wanted to probe more *deeply*. What were the forces which shaped 'The People's Preacher' in his childhood and later in life? Who were the people who had the greatest influence on him? Was he different in private to the way that he appeared in public? What was his prayer-life like and what was his attitude to the Bible? Did he have weaknesses and how were these overcome?

Seeking to get behind the headline thinking about Spurgeon and uncover the real man has been an enriching experience; I have been repeatedly challenged and humbled by Spurgeon's life and ministry. But I have also been encouraged. Most of all, I have been pointed to Jesus, again and again. My hope and prayer is that as you read these pages, this will be your experience too.

How to read this book

To help us make connections between Spurgeon and our own lives I have included two short sections at the end of each chapter, entitled 'Digging deeper' and 'Engage'. In these I have tried to reflect in more depth on Spurgeon's story and what it might have to teach us today. You could keep a notebook or journal, so you can record your discoveries and how God is speaking to you through Spurgeon's life and ministry. Also, if you're able to pray about what you are reading that would be huge help. The importance of prayer is one of the things Charles Spurgeon teaches us, so if you do spend time doing this you will already be following his example! The more thoughtfully and prayerfully you can approach the different chapters, the more I believe you will get out of them.

So, get ready to discover more about Charles Haddon Spurgeon, the People's Preacher! More importantly, get ready to catch a glimpse of the 'marvellous power' of God at work. The Victorian age *was* different to our own to be sure, but the power of God experienced then is available today, for Jesus is the same 'yesterday and today and for ever' (Hebrews 13:8). The power that transformed and shaped Spurgeon's life can therefore transform and shape our lives as well. My prayer is that we would all be changed as we see how God worked in and through the life of Charles Haddon Spurgeon. May we be faithful to God in our generation as he was faithful to God in his.

Peter Morden
Spurgeon's College
October 2009

NOTES

I have worked almost entirely from 'primary' sources – books and manuscripts from C.H. Spurgeon's time or soon after. Invaluable have been Spurgeon's sermons as published in the *Metropolitan Tabernacle Pulpit* and the massive four-volume *Autobiography* of Spurgeon (actually compiled by Spurgeon's wife, Susannah, and his private secretary, Joseph Harrald, at the close of the nineteenth century). The Heritage Room at Spurgeon's College contains thousands of original documents, many of them written by C.H. Spurgeon himself. The archive at Spurgeon's Childcare (now known simply as 'Spurgeons') in Rushden was important for the chapter on the Stockwell Orphanage. On the rare occasions I have used a secondary source – a book written about Spurgeon more recently – there is a note at the end of the chapter giving details. Quotations from primary material are verbatim, but I have occasionally modernised the punctuation to make sentences 'flow' better for the modern reader.

CHAPTER 1

Background and Family

HARLES Haddon Spurgeon was born in the small village of Kelvedon, Essex, on 19 June 1834, the first child of John and Eliza Spurgeon. At this time couples tended to have many children, partly because the infant mortality rate was so high. The hope was that at least some of them would grow into adulthood. John and Eliza would go on to have seventeen children in all, but sadly only eight – six girls and two boys – survived infancy. At the time little Charles was born the family were not well off and life was difficult. John was pastor of a small Independent chapel at Tollesbury, ten miles from Kelvedon. But he was only part-time, and received very little money from the church.

In order to make ends meet he also worked as a clerk to a coal merchant in the nearby town of Colchester, where the family moved soon after Charles's birth. When John and Eliza's second child was born the financial strain became too much. Charles was sent to live with his paternal grandparents, James and Sarah, whose home was over twenty miles away in Stambourne. Charles was only eighteen months old.

The England of the time was changing fast. The industrial revolution was in full swing and Britain was proudly spoken of as 'the workshop of the world'. But such 'progress' went hand in hand with appalling conditions for workers in the tough, grimy, over-populated cities. People laboured for long hours in dark, dingy and dangerous factories. Child labour was common. At the end of an exhausting day workers would trudge home through the narrow, airless streets to their cramped and dirty slum-like dwellings. In such miserable surroundings immorality and vice flourished. But these changes had not really touched the places in Essex where Charles grew up. Although life was hard at least the air was clean and many people pursued the simple rural way of

ABOVE
Spurgeon's father

life that had remained relatively unaltered for generations. Later, when he moved to London, Spurgeon would witness at first-hand the other, seamier side of nineteenth-century England.

Spurgeon's grandfather was also a pastor, and by the time he and Sarah took the infant Charles into their home James had already served the Independent church in Stambourne for twenty-five years. He was of Puritan stock and even dressed like an old-fashioned Puritan preacher, in knee breeches and buckled shoes. The Essex village of Stambourne was home to just 500 people. It boasted two churches (the other being Church of England) and two pubs. But it had no doctor, no chemist and no police officer. As Charles remembered it, the village was peaceful and sleepy. Grandfather James lived until 1864 but never once visited London, a mere sixty-eight miles away.

Charles lived in the Stambourne manse until he was seven. James and Sarah's unmarried daughter, Charles's Aunt Ann, still lived at home with her parents and she had a special role in caring for the boy. The years spent in Stambourne were to be formative ones in Charles's life.

Early influences

ABOVE RIGHT
Spurgeon's mother
ABOVE LEFT
Spurgeon's
paternal
grandfather
and grandmother

What were the influences which shaped the young Charles at this time? The Puritan atmosphere in which he was brought up was especially important. Today the word 'Puritan' has a bad press with many. The image of a Puritan is of a rather strict and forbidding person – someone with a long list of dos and don'ts (mostly don'ts), whose main aim in life is to spoil other people's fun. But the reality of the Puritanism which flourished in sixteenth- and seventeenth-century England was very different from this. It is true that Puritans tended to be suspicious of activities which most Christians today would regard as innocent – dancing and theatre-going, for example. But they were warm-hearted and deeply committed Christians, far removed from the joyless busybodies of popular caricature. Puritan preachers and writers studied the Bible in great depth, and produced detailed works of theology. But these works were rarely dry or dusty (although they could be extremely long). What was striking about the Puritans was the way strong doctrine was held together with a rich, deep experience of God. We might say they had a faith which touched both their heads *and* their hearts. They were also practical people who wanted to live for Christ in the real world. The Independent church at Stambourne had a long and celebrated Puritan tradition which had been upheld by a series of well-loved pastors. And James Spurgeon was proud to follow where others had led.

A large library of Puritan books had been passed down from minister to minister; these were kept in the manse. As Charles grew he would often slip into the darkened room where they were stored to look at them. He was an extremely able boy, but it is still hard to believe that he understood a great deal of what he was reading, at least to begin with, especially as he confessed he could hardly lift some of the enormous volumes. But one book in particular made an almost immediate impression. This was the Puritan classic *The Pilgrim's Progress*, written by John Bunyan and first published in the seventeenth century. The book is an allegory, or parable, of the Christian life, vividly written in a popular style. It tells the story of a young man called Christian who comes to faith in Jesus and then sets off on his pilgrimage of discipleship. On the road he meets a cast of colourful characters with names like Faithful, Hopeful and Ignorance who either help or hinder him on his journey. Christian passes through places such as Vanity Fair and Doubting Castle (where he encounters a giant called Despair) before at last he reaches his destination, the Celestial City, heaven. As he turned the pages, young Charles was captivated. The edition that he had happened upon was richly illustrated with many drawings depicting the events described in the book. He could not only begin to read Bunyan's lively prose, he could also see Christian manfully struggling through the Slough of Despond and heroically crossing the River of Death. *The Pilgrim's Progress* was a book he would treasure for the rest of his life – at one point in his ministry he claimed to have read it at least one hundred times! It was the one book which, besides the Bible, he learned to value more than any other. As a small boy images and phrases from *The Pilgrim's Progress* were burned into his consciousness and, bit by bit, his view of the Christian life was shaped.

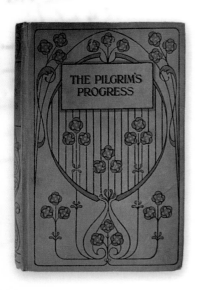

Charles's grandfather's own thinking was thoroughly moulded by works such as *The Pilgrim's Progress* and the heavier volumes of Puritan theology contained in the manse. James's preaching and general outlook were robustly biblical in an age where some ministers were beginning to question the historic truths of the Christian faith. And what he preached in the pulpit he lived out at home. Family prayers had always been an important part of Puritan spirituality. The aim was for the whole household to meet daily to read from the Bible, perhaps sing a hymn, and pray together. Charles took a full part in these times and, as he grew a little older, was often allowed to do the Bible reading. There were occasions when the young child stopped in mid-sentence, confessing that he didn't have a clue what the words he was reading meant. James was always gracious in the way he dealt with his grandson's questions. But it is likely that family prayers went on for rather longer than normal when Charles was in the house.

The boy returned to live with his parents in 1841. John and Eliza's financial situation had become a little better. Now thoroughly settled in Colchester, they were keen to welcome Charles back. Back in his parents' home, Charles continued to take part in family devotions, led by his father. These times were important in his parents' household although it seems that, given their now growing family and the pressures they were under, the routine of daily prayer together was sometimes lost. The earliest surviving piece of Charles's writing bears witness to this. At the age of eleven he produced a tiny, handwritten, 'magazine' for his family to read. In it he wrote that on Sunday 11 April 1846 a planned family prayer meeting 'was omitted', adding, 'I hope it will be resumed'. The time of prayer the following Sunday was 'very good', but the Sunday after that it was missed again, prompting Charles to write: 'What a decline'! He firmly believed, even at this age, that 'blessings come through prayer'. As we shall see, this was to be a vital emphasis for the whole of his life and ministry.

Charles did not find his return to his parents' home easy. Reflecting back on this time later in life he wrote:

> I recollect when first I left my grandfather, how grieved I was to part from him; it was the greatest sorrow of my little life. Grandfather seemed very sorry too, and we had a cry together; he did not know quite what to say to me, but he said, 'Now child, to-night, when the moon shines at Colchester, and you look at it, don't forget that it is the same moon your grandfather will be looking at from Stambourne.' And for years, as a child, I used to love the moon because I thought that my grandfather's eyes and my own somehow met there on the moon.

This story nicely illustrates the relationship Charles had with his grandfather. Even when he was living with his parents the boy would visit Stambourne as often as he could. But he grew to love his parents' home too. On Sunday evenings his mother would often speak to her children of Christian things, little talks which Charles would later say became too 'deeply settled' on his young heart to be forgotten. And she also prayed regularly, repeatedly, for her children's salvation. It is hard to exaggerate the extent to which the godly example and Christian love of his parents and grandparents influenced Charles's life.

Charles went to a local school, Stockwell House, in Colchester. Then, at the age of fourteen, he went with his brother James to a Church of England boarding school in Maidstone, Kent. None of this was free and Charles's parents sacrificed much to pay for his and his brother's education. The young Charles always did well. He was clearly extremely bright, but he did not endear himself to the Maths teacher at Maidstone, who also happened to be his uncle. The young scholar would regularly point out mistakes the teacher made – in front of the whole class. Probably his uncle was relieved when Charles left after a year to go to an Academy in Newmarket. There he had the role of an usher. As well as his own study, this meant that he also spent some of his time teaching the younger boys. This was in 1849 and Charles Spurgeon was fifteen years old.

Richard Knill's prophecy

One further incident from young Charles's childhood is worth mentioning because of the way it points to the future. When he was ten and visiting his grandparents in Stambourne, Charles met a man named Richard Knill who was staying in the manse. Knill had been a cross-cultural missionary, serving in both India and Russia. In Knill's heart, said Charles, 'burned the true missionary spirit, for he sought the souls of young and old, whenever they came in his way'. On successive days Knill took Charles into the garden of the house early in the morning to talk to him about Jesus and pray with him. At the end of the visit the missionary called the whole household – James, Sarah, Ann and Charles – together, and made the following dramatic announcement. Charles Spurgeon, declared Knill, would one day 'preach the gospel'. Furthermore, he would 'preach it to great multitudes'. An additional specific prophecy was that the child would one day preach in the then famous Surrey Chapel, in the great metropolis of London. It seemed impossible. But Knill had not finished! He told the boy that when he *did* preach at Surrey Chapel he was to ask the congregation to sing William Cowper's hymn, 'God moves in a mysterious way His wonders to perform'. An amazed Charles stammered that, if it ever *did* happen that he would preach in this chapel then, yes, he would use the hymn. But he was inclined to think of it all as an idle dream – at least to begin with. Nevertheless ten years later Knill's prophecy was indeed fulfilled. Charles Spurgeon preached at the Surrey Chapel and the emotional preacher made sure the congregation sang 'God moves in a mysterious way'. God had been as good as His word, and so had Spurgeon.

But to talk of preaching and London and large congregations is to rush ahead in the story. At the age of fifteen Charles Spurgeon was a pupil-teacher in a Newmarket school, away from home once again, and somewhat lonely. He already knew much about Christian things, for he had seen the Christian life faithfully lived by his parents and his grandparents. He knew much about church, for he had been to services since he was a tiny infant. He had even occasionally played at preaching, standing on a hay-rack to preach whilst his brother and sisters sat on hay bales as the pretend congregation. He knew about prayer, because for many years he had taken part in regular family devotions. And he knew the Bible, how to find different books and verses, better than many Christians.

However, something crucial was missing. Charles did not yet have a living faith of his own. He certainly knew he was

Charles Spurgeon … would one day 'preach the gospel'. Furthermore, he would 'preach it to great multitudes'

LEFT
Richard Knill

a sinner, and as he moved through his teenage years he grew more and more anxious concerning where he stood before God. But, although he knew much *about* Jesus, he didn't yet *know* Jesus as his own personal Saviour who would forgive him. Nevertheless, as the new year of 1850 approached this was about to change. And the story of how Charles was finally and wonderfully converted shows that God does indeed move in mysterious ways.

Digging deeper

In later years Charles Spurgeon spoke often of the 'holy influence of my early home-life'. His parents, his grandparents and his Aunt Ann were all significant figures that helped influence him for God. To be sure, as Charles grew up he had what we might call a second-hand faith. By his own testimony he didn't know Jesus personally. But, bit by bit, Charles was being prepared for the day when he would receive Christ. Perhaps especially important for young Charles were his grandfather and his mother. In the year following his eventual conversion he wrote the following lines in a letter to his mother: 'You ... have been the great means in God's hand of rendering me what I hope I am. You by God's blessing, prepared the way for the preached Word ... I love you as the preacher to my heart.'

Eliza was, said Charles, his 'praying, watching mother'. He was right to be grateful. God had used his family to prepare him not only for true conversion, but also for a lifetime's ministry and service.

Engage

If we are privileged to have children, do we pray for them and with them? Do we read the Bible with them? Perhaps most importantly of all, do we live lives in the home which truly reflect Christ and speak of His love? We can often fool people in our church fellowships regarding the quality of our lives. We can sometimes fool people in our places of work as to what we're really like, even when they see us nearly every day. We can even hide our failings

> ... although he knew much about Jesus, he didn't yet know Jesus as his own personal Saviour

from our wider family circle. But it is much harder to fool people in the home. There, people see what we're *really* like, day in, day out. They see us when we're tired, and in our weak moments. When other family members, especially children, look at us, what do they see?

Of course, not everybody is married, not everybody has children, not everybody lives in a home where all adult family members are committed to Christ. But in young Charles's life we see a number of different characters who had a role to play – grandparents, parents and his unmarried Aunt Ann. Nearly all of us know children who we can love and influence for Christ in some way. The story of the young Charles Spurgeon encourages us to depend on the Holy Spirit and use the opportunities we *do* have to do all we can. Who knows, there may be a future Spurgeon in one of our families.

But none of us is perfect; all of us fail. We don't present a consistently godly example to those close to us. Charles Spurgeon's relatives *weren't* perfect. His grandfather was, perhaps, a little too strict on occasions. His parents had a rather haphazard approach to family prayers, something which, as we have seen, young Charles was quick to point out! But God's grace and forgiveness was there for them just as it's there for us, always. And saying sorry to God, and also to people around us, is part of living an authentic Christian life. He forgives us and gives us His amazing, outrageous grace so that we can begin again.

And all of us, without exception, can do one thing. We can pray, as Charles's mother did. Who are we praying for, regularly? As you pray for children, perhaps your own, be encouraged by the example of a mother who prayed daily for her son and, after many years, saw those prayers wonderfully answered.

NEXT PAGE
A few of Spurgeon's notebooks

CHARLES HADDON SPURGEON. OCTOBER 1849

C.H. Spurgeon

Prière avant le Repas.

Répands Seigneur tes bénédiction sur les viandes dont nous allons rassasier nos corps, au nom de Jésus Christ ton Fils unique. Ainsi soit il.

Prière après le Repas.

Nous te remercions, O Seigneur de la nourriture que nous venons de recevoir au nom de Jésus Christ ton Fils unique. Ainsi soit il.

Confession Générale.

Père tout puissant et très miséricordieux nous, nous sommes égarés et détournés de tes sentiers, comme des brebis perdues nous avons trop suivi les imaginations et les convoitises de nos cœurs; nous avons transgressé tes saints commandemens, nous n'avons point fait les choses que nous aurions dû faire

CHAPTER 2

Conversion and Baptism

Conversion

O N A bitterly cold and snowy Sunday morning in January 1850,[1] the fifteen-year-old Charles Spurgeon was home from Newmarket and staying with his parents in Colchester. The weather was atrocious but Charles was determined to find somewhere to worship; indeed, he had a particular chapel in mind. Setting off on foot, he struggled through the snowstorm, bravely battling the appalling weather. But the conditions were so difficult he was unable to reach his intended destination. Instead, he turned down a narrow side street in search of shelter and came across a small chapel, one he had never visited before. Gratefully he stumbled inside, at last finding sanctuary from the biting wind and the driving snow.

The street in question was called Artillery Street, and the small chapel he'd happened upon belonged to a denomination called the Primitive Methodists. This was a Christian grouping, little heard of today, that some referred to as the 'ranters'. Spurgeon said they had a reputation for singing so loudly they made 'people's heads ache' and they were widely known for their general enthusiasm. Not that there was much enthusiasm in evidence in this particular service. Only about fifteen people had made it through the miserable weather in order to be present that morning. The chapel must have been cold and it was certainly very empty. The young Spurgeon sat alone. The service seemed to promise very little. To make matters worse (at least as far as Spurgeon was concerned) when the preacher got up to speak he announced his text in a broad Essex accent. The man

ABOVE
Exterior and interior of Primitive Methodist Chapel in Artillery Street, Colchester

seemed completely uneducated and uncouth – why, he didn't even pronounce his words properly! Spurgeon later described the preacher, somewhat unkindly, as 'really stupid'. But what happened next was to change the young visitor for ever. Charles Haddon Spurgeon was about to experience something that would make this day, for him, the most important of his whole life.

The Bible verse the preacher had chosen was Isaiah 45:22 from the Old Testament. In the old Authorised Version which Charles would have heard, this contains the words: 'Look unto me, and be ye saved, all the ends of the earth: for I am God, and there is none else.' Whilst at Stambourne Spurgeon had learnt by heart a catechism which taught basic Christian truths through the form of questions and answers. One of the questions asked 'Who was Isaiah?' and the answer young Charles learnt to repeat was: 'He was the prophet who spake more of Jesus Christ than all the rest.' What he'd previously learned in his head was now about to enter his heart. As the man began to preach he stuck closely to his text. This was largely because, Spurgeon suspected, he had little else to say. The whole congregation were encouraged to 'look to Christ' for salvation. This phrase the man repeated – over and over again.

After about ten minutes it seemed that the speaker had completely run out of ideas. But it was then that events took an unexpected and dramatic turn. Spurgeon described what happened:

[The preacher] looked at me … and I daresay, with so few present, he knew me to be a stranger. Just fixing his eyes on me, as if he knew all my heart, he said, 'Young man, you look very miserable … and you always will be miserable – miserable in life and miserable in death – if you don't obey my text. But if you obey now, this moment, you will be saved.' Then, lifting up his hands, he shouted, as only a Primitive Methodist could do, 'Young man, look to Jesus Christ. Look! Look! Look! You have nothin' to do but to look and live!'

Spurgeon was not used to preachers speaking directly to him from the pulpit! But the effect was electric. God used this simple and direct challenge, from a very ordinary speaker, to open Spurgeon's eyes. The young Spurgeon did 'look', and when he did so he saw what he called 'the wonderful sight' of 'Jesus dying for me as Saviour'. Spurgeon barely heard the rest of the sermon, but it didn't matter. God had already spoken to him, and he had responded in simple faith. The joy and wonder of his conversion that day never left him. Much later in life Spurgeon would say:

> Many days of Christian experience have passed … but there has never been one which has had the full exhilaration, the sparkling delight which that first day had. I thought I could have sprung from the seat on which I sat, and called out with the wildest of those Methodist brethren who were present, 'I am forgiven! I am forgiven! A monument of grace! A sinner saved by blood!'

In this story, two things stand out. One of them is what theologians sometimes call the 'providence' of God. Reflecting back on what had happened to him, Spurgeon did not believe that this extraordinary series of events – the snowstorm, his visit to a different chapel to the one he had planned, the preacher's direct address to the unhappy visitor – were coincidences. Rather they were what people sometimes call 'God-incidences'. God was at work here, ordering events so that His plan came to pass. The other notable point is the ordinariness of the preacher. Clearly he was nothing special as a communicator! But God had used this ordinary person to convey His extraordinary word, and applied it to a young man's heart by the power of

THE PULPIT
FROM THE
PRIMITIVE METHODIST
CHAPEL
COLCHESTER.

CONVERSION OF
C.H. SPURGEON
1850
TEXT
'Look unto Me and be ye Saved'

His Holy Spirit. This is something God still does today.

So, the Spurgeon who, at the close of the service, made his way home through the now deeply lying snow was a new person. His mother immediately noticed that something had happened. Her son was different; his face had changed – he was no longer miserable or despondent! Later, Charles sat up into the night with his father as they talked of his new-found faith. They had spoken of Christian things previously, of course, but this time it was different. Topics such as forgiveness and grace came alive for Charles as they never had before. He had truly looked to Christ and now, for the first time, he could *really* see what the Christian faith was all about. The chapter in Spurgeon's *Autobiography* that speaks of these events is called 'The Great Change'. The title was well chosen. The young Charles *had* changed and the change was great indeed. His life would never be the same again.

Baptism

John and Eliza were obviously overjoyed at their son's conversion. But a decision Charles made later that year was against their wishes, and also those of his grandfather, James. For, on Friday 3 May 1850, Charles Spurgeon was baptised as a believer, by immersion.

On his return to Newmarket, Charles had joined a Congregational church. This was the denomination of his parents and grandparents, which practised infant baptism. This much his family would have warmly approved of. But Charles had earlier learnt about believers' baptism at school and, as he studied the Scriptures, he was convinced that this was the right way to be baptised. Never one to go against his convictions, Charles was determined that he would be baptised as a believer, and without delay. His parents were not best pleased, especially to begin with. But, after a brief tussle, they gave their blessing, which Charles as a dutiful Victorian son had sought. Still, his mother told him that, although she had repeatedly prayed her son would become a Christian, she had never once prayed that he would become a Baptist. Charles responded in the words of Ephesians 3:20: God had not only answered her prayers but had been pleased to do abundantly more than she had asked or thought. His mother's reply has not been recorded!

The nearest Baptist minister Charles could find who was willing to baptise him was a Reverend William Cantlow, from Isleham, about eight miles from Newmarket. On the day of the baptism the young Spurgeon rose early and prepared himself with two hours of prayer and 'quiet dedication to God'. A further two to three hours were spent walking to the spot near Isleham where he, together with two women, would be baptised. And the spot was not a chapel building, but the banks of the River Lark, at a place called Isleham Ferry. This baptism was to take place in the open air.

A number of people had gathered to watch the baptisms. Some were supportive chapel-goers but almost certainly others were just curious onlookers. There were many people in boats as well as those standing on the banks of the river. It was a cold day and Spurgeon initially felt timid and anxious. He was asked to help the two women into the water, and lead them out into the river where the minister was waiting for them in a spot where the water was deep enough for the baptisms to take place. But Spurgeon nervously declined. The fact was he had never actually *seen* a service of believers' baptism before and was 'afraid of making some mistake'. But his own description of what happened when it was his turn to be baptised is vivid and powerful:

> The wind blew down the river with a cutting blast as my turn came to wade into the flood; but after I had walked a few steps, and noted the people on the ferry-boat, and in boats, and on either shore, I felt as if heaven and earth and hell might all gaze upon me, for I was not

LEFT
Isleham Ferry on the River Lark, where Spurgeon was baptised

ashamed, then and there, to own myself a follower of the Lamb. My timidity was washed away; it floated down the river into the sea, and must have been devoured by the fishes, for I have never felt anything of the kind since. Baptism also loosed my tongue, and from that day it has never been quiet.

Spurgeon had stepped out in faith, and God had met him in the waters of baptism.

Growth

One further event (or, more accurately, series of events) is worthy of note. Both before and after his conversion, Spurgeon spent time with a cook at his Newmarket school. The cook's name was Mary King and she was a devout Christian. She had no formal theological training but she knew the Scriptures deeply and understood Christian doctrine clearly. She was willing to spend many hours with Charles, meeting with him regularly to discuss the great truths of the Christian faith. These included the cross of Christ and the sheer grace of God – the wonderful, undeserved love that He lavishes on His children. Mary King was a Calvinist: she strongly emphasised the sovereignty of God, whilst not minimising the truth that humans are also responsible for their own actions. This was also what Spurgeon had come to believe (in line with the vast majority of the Puritans).

Spurgeon lapped up the help he received from Mary King and later said that, apart from his family, the 'first lessons I ever had in theology' were from her. What particularly impressed him about Mary was the way she lived what she believed. Her knowledge of Christian doctrine was impressive, but it was not head knowledge only – it impacted the whole of her life. She was, he said, 'a godly experienced woman, from whom I learned far more than I did from the minister of the chapel we attended'. Spurgeon was growing in knowledge and love of God. The stage was set for further remarkable developments in his life.

🔖 Digging deeper

One of the things that is striking about Spurgeon's conversion and early Christian experience is the way God used ordinary people to touch the young man's life. The man who urged a handful of faithful worshippers and one very unhappy stranger to 'look to Christ' one freezing January morning was clearly not a gifted preacher. In fact, amazingly, no one to this day is really sure who the man was. As Spurgeon's fame grew, at least three people claimed to be the speaker, but Charles said he recognised none of them. Historians think the most likely candidate was Robert Eaglen, a minister who preached regularly in the little Primitive Methodist chapels in the Colchester and Ipswich area. But when Eaglen was presented to Spurgeon, some years after the event, Charles said: 'This is not the man' (it's possible that age had changed Eaglen's appearance quite considerably). The identity of the preacher will probably never be known with absolute certainty. But God knows, and He used this ordinary man and his faltering, stammering, message to convert a man who was to become the best known popular preacher in Victorian Britain.

William Cantlow, the man who baptised Spurgeon, had been a missionary in Jamaica, but had returned to England to pastor the small Isleham church, a position he held for thirty-two years. He was a faithful minister for sure, and loved by his people, but the only reason anyone has heard of him today is because he was the man who baptised Spurgeon – a fact that is proudly written on his gravestone. William Cantlow was a dedicated if rather unremarkable Baptist pastor. But Spurgeon never forgot Cantlow's warmth, welcome and ministry. Like the anonymous Primitive Methodist preacher, Cantlow was another ordinary man who was greatly used by an extraordinary God.

And what of Mary King? She was never a pastor, never preached and never led a church service. In the branch of the Baptist Church she was committed to, these things would have been impossible for a woman. We might say she was the most ordinary of these three people – almost certainly she would have said this herself. But her

She was ... 'a godly experienced woman, from whom I learned far more than I did from the minister of the chapel we attended' grasp of Christian truth was great, and quietly and effectively she poured what she knew into her young friend. Her deep love for God and His ways created a lasting impression, and Spurgeon did not forget her. In later life she grew increasingly frail and had little money. Spurgeon the famous preacher heard of her situation and stepped in, supporting her financially until her death. Spurgeon always remembered his debt to her, as he remembered the others who had helped him as he took his first steps as a new Christian.

Engage

Looking back over the examples of the Methodist preacher, Baptist minister William Cantlow and, perhaps especially, Mary King, there is a great lesson to be learned. God uses ordinary Christian people and can do great things through them. The application to our own lives is not hard to see. We may feel we are not especially gifted and that we don't have great opportunities to serve Christ; we'll never be Charles Spurgeon, or Billy Graham, or for that matter anyone that people have particularly heard of. But God uses ordinary Christians who are faithful to Him in the small things in life. Be encouraged about this and stay faithful! Who knows who God is going to bring across your path, and how He is going to use you to bring glory to Him?

NOTE

1 Spurgeon recalled the exact date of his conversion as being 6 January 1850. But a number of historians now think he was mistaken and that actually it was on the Sunday after – 13 January 1850. If you want to follow this up see L. Drummond, *Spurgeon: Prince of Preachers* (Grand Rapids, Michigan: Kregel, 1992), pp.114–131.

CHAPTER 3

The Boy Preacher
of the Fens

ITHIN a month of his conversion Spurgeon began to keep a diary, and on the first page he wrote the following prayer of commitment:

CONSECRATION

O great and unsearchable God, who knowest my heart, and triest all my ways; with a humble dependence upon the support of Thy Holy Spirit, I yield myself up to Thee as Thine own reasonable sacrifice, I return to Thee Thine own. I would be for ever, unreservedly, perpetually Thine. Whilst I am on earth I would serve Thee; and may I enjoy Thee and praise Thee for ever! Amen.

1 February 1850 Charles Haddon Spurgeon

All the Christians of the time would have spoken to God using what we might term 'old-fashioned' language. To address God in any other way would have been regarded as irreverent, but it can seem strange to many of us today. But even as we read the unfamiliar wording, we can pick up the utter passion the young Spurgeon had for his Saviour. There were no half-measures with him. As a Christian he wasn't content to be a pew-filler or even just mildly committed. Drawing his strength from God, Charles Spurgeon was determined to be out and out for his Lord. This wholehearted commitment was worked out in practice in the years immediately after his conversion.

The boy preacher

Spurgeon wasted no time putting his new-found faith into practice. As we've already seen, soon after he became a Christian he joined a Congregational church at Newmarket and was baptised as a believer at Isleham Ferry. Almost immediately he started teaching in the Sunday school at his Newmarket church and distributing tracts – Christian leaflets – in the town. But this was only the beginning.

On 17 June 1850 he left Newmarket in order to take up a teaching post at a Cambridge school and continue his own studies. There he joined St Andrew's Street Baptist Church, one of the city's historic churches. Every week he taught at the afternoon Sunday school. His lessons were so popular that many adults began attending. Soon the classes were packed. Charles had written to his father back in Colchester about his longing to preach. His wish was about to be granted – and in an unusual way.

In Cambridge there was something called a Preacher's Association which was based at St Andrew's Street. This association provided speakers for small chapels and meeting houses in the villages and hamlets surrounding the city. The man who decided who preached where and when was a certain James Vinter, known affectionately to many as Bishop Vinter. According to Spurgeon, Vinter was a 'venerable' and 'genial soul' with a 'warm heart' and 'kindly manner'. Spurgeon was not part of the association, but the quality of his Sunday school teaching had come to Vinter's attention. The 'Bishop' wanted to use Spurgeon as one of his

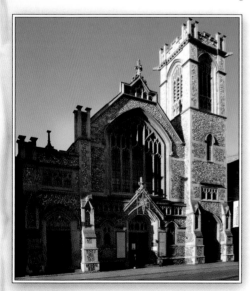

preachers, but he correctly guessed that the young man, despite his earnest desire to preach, would be too shy to accept a direct invitation. So, Vinter hatched a plan. He approached Spurgeon one Saturday and asked if he would be willing to go the next day to a place called Teversham, where there was going to be a service. But all Spurgeon was told was that a certain unnamed young man was going to preach there, someone who was 'not much used to services'. This young man, Spurgeon was further informed, would 'very likely' be glad of some company. Spurgeon accepted the invitation. He was more than happy to accompany this unknown young preacher on the long walk to Teversham.

Spurgeon's suspicions should have been aroused when he met his companion, and saw that the man in question was several years older than he was. After they had gone some distance Spurgeon expressed the hope that his new friend would 'feel the presence of God while preaching'. The other man was amazed! *He* had never

preached in his life and wasn't going to start now – it was *Spurgeon* who was to be the preacher; at least, that's what Vinter had told him! Spurgeon remembered the words Vinter had used when he'd asked him to go to Teversham, and saw how craftily they'd been constructed. He was the young man 'not much used to services' that Vinter had been talking about. Spurgeon was not happy!

As the pair continued towards Teversham, Spurgeon protested that he really ought not to preach. Just like his older companion, he had never spoken at a church service before and, anyway, he was quite unprepared. But the older man was insistent: 'Why not give them one of your Sunday school talks?' It soon became clear that, if Spurgeon didn't agree to preach, there would be no message for the people of Teversham that day. At last young Charles accepted. The two walked on in silence while Spurgeon decided on a text, put together some thoughts, and prayed hard. Probably he also took a moment to think through what he might say to 'Bishop Vinter' after they had returned to Cambridge.

The people at Teversham didn't have a special church building – they met in a small thatched cottage, and it was there that a few farm labourers and their wives had gathered. Spurgeon's text was

LEFT
St Andrew's Street Baptist Church today
ABOVE
Cottage at Teversham in which Spurgeon preached his first sermon

to be 1 Peter 2.7: 'Unto you therefore which believe he is precious' (AV). He had resolved, in his first-ever sermon, to 'tell out the story of the cross'. After some singing, some prayers and a Bible reading the time came for Spurgeon to speak.

> How long or how short it was I cannot now remember. It was not half such a task as I had feared it would be, but I was glad to see my way to a fair conclusion, and to the giving out of the last hymn. To my own delight, I had not broken down, nor stopped short in the middle, nor been destitute of ideas, and the desired haven was in view. I made finish, and took up the hymn book. But, to my astonishment, an aged voice cried out, 'Bless your dear heart, how old are you?' My very solemn reply was, 'You must wait till the service is over before making such enquiries. Let us sing.'

After the service had officially ended, Spurgeon was asked again, 'How old are you?'

'I am under sixty,' he responded.

'Yes, and under sixteen,' was the reply (actually Spurgeon was just sixteen, but it was a good guess).

Spurgeon's final answer was: 'Never mind my age, think of the Lord Jesus and his preciousness.'

Spurgeon had not only reached the end of the service without mishap, he had pointed people to Christ and His cross. A later sermon outline which Spurgeon produced on the same text begins with the following note: 'This was the theme of the first sermon I ever preached; I hope it is my theme now, and ever shall be.' Spurgeon had preached for the first time. He would do much better in future, but he would never find a better subject. It had a good beginning and it was also how he was determined to go on.

Unsurprisingly, it wasn't long before Spurgeon was in great demand as a preacher. The invitations came so regularly that he would sometimes take services three times on a Sunday and every night of the week as well! Many of his engagements were in outlying villages which were not easy to reach. He frequently had to walk three, five, or even eight miles in all weathers, along narrow tracks and across muddy fields, in order to reach his destination, which was often a cottage or barn. When he travelled in the evening it was usually in darkness, with only a flickering lantern to light the way. When it rained Spurgeon also donned a pair of waterproof leggings. On one occasion, Spurgeon struggled through a storm only to find, when he finally reached the village, that the agreed meeting place was deserted – the villagers had assumed the weather was so bad that no one would arrive to take their service. Ignoring the pouring rain, Spurgeon went from house to house knocking on the doors and successfully gathered a congregation.

It was quite obvious that he was a gifted preacher. But people also noticed his dedication to God and his sheer enthusiasm. This and his age. Soon the young man had become known throughout the local Fenland district as 'the boy preacher of the Fens'. Spurgeon's initial prayer of consecration was being worked out in practical action. He had been faithful in small things. Now God was about to open up a new sphere of service for him.

The boy pastor

One place where Spurgeon preached was the village of Waterbeach, about six miles from Cambridge. The village was somewhat unusual in that it did boast a small, thatched Chapel building, and recently they had had a minister. The church could not support him, however, and the man felt compelled to leave. When Spurgeon first preached there, in October 1851, Waterbeach Chapel was at a low ebb. Spurgeon was immediately invited to return for the next two Sundays. He ended up staying for the next two years having accepted the 'call' to be the church's minister. At the age of seventeen the boy preacher became the boy pastor.

By any standards, Spurgeon's short ministry at Waterbeach was remarkable. In his *Autobiography* he describes a certain village which was 'notorious for its drunkenness and profanity'. Robbery was common. The inhabitants lived in abject poverty, 'degradation' and 'misery'. But, said Spurgeon, in a few years this particular place had been turned 'upside down' through the preaching of a young lad who was 'earnest' for souls. The little thatched chapel was packed to the rafters Sunday by Sunday. Robberies and 'villainies of every kind' had ceased, for those who had committed them were themselves 'in the house of God, rejoicing to hear of Christ crucified'. Not only were the lives of individuals being changed, but the life of the village as a whole was being transformed. Where formerly there was 'drunkenness' and 'debauchery', men and women now 'went forth to labour with joyful hearts, singing the praises of the ever-living God'. It was an extraordinary transformation; indeed, it sounded like fiction. But in the course of his description Spurgeon revealed what the readers of the *Autobiography* had no doubt already guessed. Waterbeach was the village, Spurgeon himself was the preacher, and the story was true.

Spurgeon was clearly concerned that his description of events would be regarded by his readers as an exaggeration, but he was quick to reassure them that this was not the case. There is other evidence which supports Spurgeon's own account. For example, there is a letter from a deacon at Waterbeach to Spurgeon's father, written in March 1852. This spoke of people unable to get into services because the building was already too crammed. If Spurgeon's father were to visit Waterbeach, the deacon insisted, he would find this account was 'not exaggerated'. Rather, he would be more likely to exclaim, 'the half was not told me'. Given this, and also what God would later accomplish through Spurgeon in London, there is no real reason to doubt the preacher's own enthusiastic portrayal of events.

What was the message Spurgeon preached which, under God, had caused such a turnaround in village life? Six books of sermon notes survive, and are kept in the Heritage Room at Spurgeon's College. Some of the sermon outlines are also reproduced in the *Autobiography*. These notes show that Spurgeon preached the same strong doctrine with the same practical application that he had learned in the Stambourne manse and from the Newmarket

cook, Mary King. Spurgeon was clearly gifted and extraordinarily committed. But he believed it was the message he preached – together with the power of God confirming the truth to people's hearts – that was key to what was happening.

Although these early sermons only survive in the form of brief outlines they do give some sense of the message and the way it was conveyed. One sermon was on Luke 19:41. This is the verse which records how Jesus wept over Jerusalem as He approached the city on the first Palm Sunday. Spurgeon entitled the sermon

'The Redeemer's Tears Over Sinners'. His handwritten notes give enough detail to show that he preached an astonishingly vivid, though simple message on the tears of Jesus. The Lord Jesus wept over sinful Jerusalem because, despite many privileges, the people there refused to turn to God. But, said Spurgeon, those living in Waterbeach had also known many privileges and they too were sinful. Why, a number of those sitting there in chapel that morning had yet to turn to Christ! Didn't the Lord Jesus shed tears for them as well? Spurgeon was sure that He did. One can only imagine the scene with Spurgeon lifting his arms and dramatically declaring that Jesus wept 'over Waterbeach and over this congregation'. In straightforward terms Spurgeon proceeded to spell out the compassion of Christ for them, proclaim the message of the gospel, and urge all those present to respond with repentance and faith in Christ. Spurgeon recalled that during his ministry at Waterbeach many villagers wept as they turned to Christ and received Him. Were at least some of these in response to this gospel sermon on the tears of Jesus?

Spurgeon's ministry began with only forty people attending chapel regularly. After two years of this sort of preaching, upwards of four hundred regularly came. The space problem was partly solved by leaving the doors and windows of the building open so that those unable to get inside could hear. The aisles and even the minister's vestry were used. Revival had broken out in a small village in the rural Cambridgeshire fens.

Despite these remarkable scenes at Waterbeach, Spurgeon the pastor continued with his regular teaching work at his Cambridge school. Even with the phenomenal growth in chapel attendance the church still struggled to pay him, for the members were almost universally poor. When the work grew to such an extent that Spurgeon had no choice but to give up his day job, it was a constant struggle to make ends meet. The church agreed to pay him £45 a year as a stipend, but this on its own was not sufficient for him to live on, as he still had to pay for board and lodging in Cambridge. The Waterbeach people did what they could to help him, often giving him farm produce such as bread and meat, which he sometimes used to pay his landlady. Spurgeon did not think that a pig was ever killed in the village without him receiving part of it as a gift. They were also generous with their hospitality and fed him well on Sundays. Spurgeon survived and the church continued to flourish.

'The Lord's hand behind the maid's mistake'

The young man's obvious calling as a preacher and pastor led to a pressing question: shouldn't he go away to college to train? Many thought so, and it was probably the deacons at St Andrew's Street who arranged for Spurgeon to meet a Dr Joseph Angus, the Principal of Regent's Park College, with a view to him training there. This was a college which prepared men for Baptist ministry – in those days no women trained – and it was then based in Stepney in London. Angus happened to be in Cambridge for a few days in February 1852. The meeting between college principal and prospective student was duly arranged to take place at a large house owned by a Mr MacMillan, a publisher and grandfather of the future British prime minister, Harold MacMillan. The scene was set for what seemed the obvious next step in the 'boy preacher's' ministry.

But Spurgeon appears to have gone to the meeting with Angus with a heavy heart. He did not want to leave Waterbeach, which he had come to love and, probably, he did not want to go to London, which he recognised would be very different to the rural fens. But he was open to God's call. Arriving at the imposing house at exactly the right time, he was shown into a room by the maid. Here he dutifully waited for Angus to arrive. Two hours later he was still waiting! Spurgeon had not asked the reason for the long delay. There must be a reason for it and it would, thought Spurgeon, have been rude to enquire. But after the two hours had ticked by he felt he could wait no longer. Nervously he rang the bell only to find out the truth of what had happened. Angus had arrived soon after Spurgeon, but the maid had not realised that the two men

The aisles and even the minister's vestry were used. Revival had broken out . . .

were there to meet one another. The tutor had been shown into a completely different room, where he too had waited. Both men were in the house at the same time but neither of them knew it! What was worse, by the time Spurgeon had summoned the maid, Angus had left to catch his train back to London, no doubt fuming that the impudent young man he had come to meet had failed to keep his appointment.

At that moment Spurgeon confessed to being rather 'disappointed'. No doubt Angus felt the same! But Spurgeon's disappointment, at least, would not remain. That afternoon, as he was out walking, he believed that God spoke to him clearly through the words of Jeremiah 45:5: '... seekest thou great things for thyself? seek them not' (AV). This he took as a word from the Lord to abandon the possibility of a college education, and 'stay with the poor but loving people' to whom he ministered. A period of further reflection strengthened his conviction. It was his duty to remain – for a while at least. Spurgeon came to believe that the 'Lord's hand' had been behind the 'maid's mistake'.

But, as it happened, London could not be delayed for ever. On the last Sunday of November 1853 Spurgeon received a letter with a postmark showing that it had come from England's capital city. It was an invitation for him to preach at the well-known New Park Street Chapel in Southwark. One of Spurgeon's deacons at Waterbeach, reading the letter, guessed with dismay that the church at New Park Street, who were then without a minister, were interested in 'calling' their pastor. Spurgeon himself thought there must be some mistake. Was the letter perhaps meant for another preacher called Spurgeon, who was a minister in nearby Norfolk? Writing to tentatively accept the invitation to speak at New Park Street on a Sunday in December, Spurgeon was concerned in case the London church was unaware of his age. He said: 'My last birthday was only my nineteenth. If you think my years would unqualify me for your pulpit ... then do not let me come.' New Park Street quickly responded, making it clear that not only had the letter reached the right Spurgeon, but that they were well aware of his age. The period of Spurgeon's life which earned him the title 'the boy preacher of the Fens' was about to come to an end.

🛈 Digging deeper

In this chapter we've seen how Spurgeon's prayer of consecration began to be worked out in practice. The first thing that Spurgeon was clear about was that he needed to get fully engaged in the life of a local church. First in Newmarket, then in Cambridge and finally in Waterbeach, he threw himself into church life.

Spurgeon's commitment was further worked out in various ways. He taught at his Cambridge school to the best of his ability, always seeking to be a witness in his place of work. He gave himself to evangelistic work in the community. This led on to Sunday school teaching and, finally, preaching and teaching in local churches, especially at Waterbeach. Within three years of his conversion he was pastor of a thriving church, had seen many lives changed and a whole community transformed for the gospel. The years 1850-53 were for Spurgeon a whirlwind of activity in the cause of Christ. They were also preparation for what was soon to come.

All of this did not come without tensions and trouble. The struggle to survive financially was one such difficulty. Spurgeon's diary, which was effectively a spiritual journal, also reveals that there were times early in his Christian life when he felt low and when God seemed distant. Similarly, there were times when he did not find the Christian life easy. 'How feeble I am,' he confessed on 15 May 1850, 'I am not able to keep myself near to God. I am compelled to acknowledge my own deadness.' On 11 June he wrote that prayer 'seemed like a labour'. Still later he wrote, in an undated entry, that he had gone through a time when spiritual 'storms' had 'raged' around him. Given the remarkable progress of Spurgeon's ministry during this period, this glimpse into his inner life surprises

LEFT
Young Spurgeon preaching

us. Perhaps the tendency to depression with which Spurgeon would battle in later years was already troubling him. But whatever he was feeling, his commitment to Christ remained. He was determined to follow his Lord, as he put it, both in 'shade as well as sunshine'.

⛶ Engage

Once again, applications to our own lives are not hard to see. To begin with, we know that sometimes we don't fully commit to a local church or fellowship. Spurgeon would have strongly disapproved and would urge us to get involved.

Most importantly, we need to be challenged by Spurgeon's total commitment to God.

Relying on God the Holy Spirit, Spurgeon was determined to serve his Lord, holding nothing back. Near the end of his ministry in Waterbeach he wrote the following:

> I have a good sphere of labour here, but I want to do more, if possible. There is a great field, and the labourers must work with all their might. I often wish I were in China, India, or Africa that I might preach, preach, preach all day long. It would be sweet to die preaching. But I want more of the Holy Spirit; I do not feel enough – no not half enough – of his divine energy. 'Come Holy Spirit, come!'

You may not be called to overseas cross-cultural mission work (although God may be asking you to consider this); you may not be called to preach (although God may be challenging you to consider this, too). But you and I are most definitely called to give ourselves totally to God and to pray, along with Spurgeon, 'Come Holy Spirit, come!' The challenge, then, is for us to give ourselves afresh to God, relying on His help. If we do this then who knows what God might do through us?

CHAPTER 4

The Preaching Sensation of London

his esteem

descending

y brings lo

g praise

preparet

e mountai

e young

orse : he

ar him, in those

e former section is

it is seen in nature

espond to Jehovah."

r thanks.   All that

dness ; therefore let

HE London which Spurgeon travelled to, in order to fulfil his engagement at New Park Street, was completely different from the places he had known. Stambourne and Waterbeach were rural through and through. They were quiet, little seemed to change and the general pace of life was slow. Even Colchester, Newmarket and Cambridge couldn't compare. The centre of London was only some sixty miles from Waterbeach. But it might have been a world away.

At that time London, with a population of three million, was the largest city in the world. It was a place of contrasts. On the one hand it was at the hub of the British Empire – a centre of government and a hive of industry and commerce. Some areas of the capital were prosperous and rich. Everyone knew of London's importance. But there was another side to the city. Mostly it was cramped, noisy and dirty. Sanitation was poor, with the River Thames little more than an open sewer. The London smogs – where mist combined with the ever-present smoke to form a thick, choking fog – were common. When these pea-soupers descended, visibility could be cut almost to nothing. Disease was endemic; crime was rife; poverty was widespread. It was this seedier Dickensian side of London which struck Spurgeon when he arrived by train on the Saturday evening, the day before he was due to preach. On this first night spent in the city, Spurgeon thought that, in comparison with London, Cambridge and Waterbeach seemed like the Garden of Eden.

A call to London

The weekend appeared to promise little for the young country preacher. None of the New Park Street members had offered Spurgeon a bed for the night, but had instead arranged for him to stay in a boarding house some distance away from the chapel. Spurgeon's fellow boarders were unfriendly and he felt utterly alone. The room he was shown to was the size of a cupboard. There was barely space for him to kneel to pray. Worse still, the tiny room was right at the front of the house. Throughout the night Spurgeon was disturbed by the noisy clatter of the horse-drawn cabs going past his window, as the gas lamps continued to burn and flicker in the cold December darkness. He said: 'On the narrow bed I tossed in solitary misery, and found no pity.' Spurgeon was thoroughly despondent.

In the morning he walked through the narrow, grimy streets – what he later described as a 'dreary wilderness of brick' – to reach the chapel. New Park Street was a church with a significant history. Previous ministers, still well known at the time, were John Gill and John Rippon. The hymn book which was in use in most English Baptist churches, including at Waterbeach, had been compiled by the famous Rippon. But the present state of the church was much less impressive than its past.

A major part of the problem was the area surrounding New Park Street. The congregation had previously met in a chapel in Carter Lane near London Bridge, but that building had been demolished in 1830 to make way for new roads. The church had received compensation, but the relocation to New Park Street had been little short of a disaster. Although the new building was well constructed, the area in which it was situated was, to put it mildly, uninviting. This chapel was close to Southwark Bridge just south of the Thames. Immediately surrounding it was a mix of slum housing and, increasingly, industry – enormous breweries, vinegar factories and boiler works. The huge buildings billowed clouds of acrid smoke into the already polluted atmosphere. One former minister of the church wrote that he had hardly ever seen a more 'dingy' and 'repelling' district.

ABOVE New Park Street Chapel

RIGHT: Spurgeon in the pulpit at New Park Street Chapel

OPPOSITE Young Spurgeon

Spurgeon himself described it as 'dim, dirty and destitute, and frequently flooded by the river at high tides'.

To make matters worse, a toll had to be paid to cross Southwark Bridge, discouraging visitors from the northern half of the city. This supremely unpromising site had combined with a succession of short pastorates to leave the church in a state which left it well short of its former glories. Spurgeon's observation that 'the clouds gathered heavily, and no sunlight appeared' was a comment both on the Southwark skyline and also on the condition of the church.

The congregation that came together to hear Spurgeon on his first Sunday at New Park Street was, therefore, small in number and dispirited. Spurgeon preached on James 1:17 and God as the 'Father of lights' (AV). A sure sign that something was happening was that the evening congregation was significantly larger than the morning's – people had enthusiastically told friends and family about the lively young preacher. At the end of the day, the deacons were besieged by people urging them to invite Spurgeon to preach again.

But not everyone was so taken with the visitor. One younger worshipper, Miss Susannah Thompson, was distinctly unimpressed. Susannah attended in the evening. She viewed the speaker as a rather vulgar country yokel, with 'badly trimmed' hair and dressed in ill-fitting clothes. What's more, he had, as far as she was concerned, an unfortunate manner of speaking and a hint of arrogance about him. Certainly he was quite unsuitable for the church *she* attended! But, as we shall discover later, Susannah Thompson's views on the young preacher would eventually change.

As for Spurgeon himself, he was considerably happier at the end of the Sunday than he had been at the beginning. He was persuaded to return to New Park Street again, and this time the church offered him hospitality! Spurgeon preached on three different Sundays in January 1854. His church in Waterbeach realised what was happening and there were many tears. At the end of the month Spurgeon accepted a 'call' from the London church to be their pastor, initially for a short trial period, although it was pretty clear to all concerned that the arrangement would become permanent. On hearing the news someone who knew him from Colchester was sceptical, and not a little bitter: 'Charlie Spurgeon has been invited to London, and they are actually going to pay him £150 a year!' The acquaintance would have been incredulous had he known that very soon Spurgeon would be the preaching sensation of the capital.

A ministry grows

With Spurgeon's move to London his career veered, as one modern writer has put it, from the 'unusual to the exceptional'.[1] Within two months he was able to write to friends from his new and comfortable lodgings that 'my chapel, though large, is crowded; the aisles are blocked up, and every niche is packed as full as possible.'

Spurgeon preached the same gospel he had proclaimed at Waterbeach, and with the same effect. Although full of strong theology and biblical content it was simple and direct, in the language of the people. It was also lively and dramatic, in stark contrast to the rather correct and stodgy messages London churchgoers were used to hearing. Others spoke in a dull monotone; Spurgeon's voice was perfect for preaching – clear, strong and engaging. Other ministers read their sermons; Spurgeon preached from just a few notes, and with great freedom. He put so much into his sermons that at the end of preaching he would often be completely drained – physically, emotionally and spiritually. More than once he had to be helped from the platform, so exhausted was he by his efforts. The people had seen and heard nothing like it. And each week they braved the grime and smell of the chapel's surroundings to hear more.

Quickly, Spurgeon began to attract reams of comment from the London newspapers, most of it hostile. Spurgeon, they said, was like a comet which blazed across the sky – he would burn brightly for a while but would disappear just as quickly as he had appeared. Yes, Spurgeon was the flavour of the month, but he would soon be forgotten. Others were more personal in their criticism. Spurgeon

Spurgeon, they said ... would disappear just as quickly as he had appeared was 'uncouth' and 'loutish', no more than a jumped-up country bumpkin. One correspondent even accused him of blasphemy because of his style of preaching.

Spurgeon was undoubtedly sensitive, and at least some of this sort of talk wounded him. He was, he believed, suffering for the sake of Christ. But the predictions that Spurgeon's popularity would quickly fade were to be proved spectacularly wrong. Far more accurate were the words of a well-known actor and playwright, Sheridan Knowles, who had heard Spurgeon within a few weeks of the preacher's arrival in London. According to Knowles, the 'Cambridgeshire lad' was the 'most wonderful preacher in the world'. Knowles said he would have been willing to offer Spurgeon a 'fortune' to appear in one of his plays (the actor knew that Spurgeon would never have accepted). Spurgeon's name, declared Knowles in suitably dramatic tones, will 'be known everywhere' and his sermons 'will be translated into many languages of the world'.

Even given the excitement Spurgeon was causing in his first few months in London, this seemed far-fetched. But it was yet another 'prophecy' about the young preacher which was to come true.

The 1854 cholera epidemic

Spurgeon not only gave himself to preaching but also to pastoral work. As far as this was concerned he was soon to face what would be his sternest test yet. Towards the end of 1854, Spurgeon's district was hit by an outbreak of the deadly disease cholera. Spread by contaminated water or food (in Southwark it could have been either) this was a particularly virulent strain. One by one, different members of his congregation began to get sick – and to die. Spurgeon visited from house to house, gave what comfort and encouragement he could, and took numerous funeral services. Because he threw himself into this work, others in the area with no connection to New Park Street began to plead with him to visit. The work was exhausting, and unsurprisingly he began to fear

Knowles said he would have been willing to offer Spurgeon a 'fortune' to appear in one of his plays

RIGHT
Susannah
Thompson

for his own safety. How long would it be before cholera caught up with *him*? He said, 'My friends seemed to be falling one by one and I felt or fancied that I was sickening like those around me ... My burden was heavier than I could bear. I was ready to sink under it.' Spurgeon was still only twenty years of age.

Not for the first or last time, God spoke to Spurgeon through His Word, the Bible. As he was returning home from yet another funeral he saw a paper, pasted up in the window of a shop. As he looked more closely he saw that it wasn't an advertisement, but some verses of Scripture. In bold handwriting were written the words from Psalm 91:9–10 (AV):

> Because thou hast made the LORD, which is my refuge, even the most High, thy habitation; There shall no evil befall thee, neither shall any plague come nigh thy dwelling.

The effect upon Spurgeon was, he said, 'immediate'. God had spoken directly to his heart and he was able to continue his work with the fear of evil gone. The 'plague' did pass, although not before having exacted a terrible toll, both on the church and the wider community. But Spurgeon himself, who had been in such close contact with the dead and dying, did not get sick. He was utterly convinced that God had protected him.

Marriage

Spurgeon would also remember 1854 for an altogether happier reason than the cholera outbreak. If Susannah Thompson had been singularly unimpressed at her first sight of the young country preacher, by now she was having second thoughts. Susannah was not at this time a member at New Park Street. She had made a commitment to Christ sometime earlier and attended the church fairly regularly. But she was, as she admitted herself, in a 'backslidden' state –

struggling to live out her Christian faith or feel any warmth in her heart towards God. But, as she heard Spurgeon's powerful sermons, her feelings began to change – both towards God and the preacher.

Spurgeon gave her an illustrated copy of his favourite book, *The Pilgrim's Progress*, which he inscribed with the words: 'Miss Thompson – with desires for her progress in the blessed pilgrimage.' He also met with her on a number of occasions and led her, as she put it, 'to the cross of Christ for the peace and pardon my weary soul was looking for'. Even later, Susannah was certain that Spurgeon's concern for her at this stage was purely pastoral. According to her, their 'friendship steadily grew', but she was still surprised when Spurgeon revealed that he had feelings for her.

Susannah and Charles were both part of a large party from the church who attended the opening of the Crystal Palace, near Sydenham, on 10 June 1854. The palace had originally stood in Hyde Park. There it had housed the Great Exhibition which had showcased the best industrial products from Britain and around the world. The relocation to south-east London of the great glass

ABOVE LEFT–RIGHT: Spurgeon's wife Susannah later in life; Engraving from an edition of the *Pilgrim's Progress*, published in London, 1778; Newspaper cutting about how to choose a spouse structure known in cockney rhyming slang as 'The Screaming Alice' was a major event. The New Park Street party were part of a large crowd. As they sat waiting for a procession to pass by, Charles handed Susannah a book with the rather unpromising title *Proverbial Philosophy*. But the book included a chapter on marriage with some advice on the subject: 'Seek a good wife ... think of her, and pray for her well.'

Having pointed out these lines to the blushing Susannah, Charles followed up with the words: 'Do you pray for him who is to be *your* husband?' This rather vague and roundabout way of declaring his love was still enough to cause Susannah to experience a 'fast-beating heart'. Later, Charles would make his feelings known in a more conventional way!

The next year saw great progress, both in Susannah's Christian life and in their love for one another. They continued to do their courting at Crystal Palace, regularly strolling together among the crowds. Charles baptised Susannah as a believer, before a still largely unsuspecting congregation, on 1 February 1855. Their engagement was sealed by a gift (from her to him) of a complete set of John Calvin's *Commentaries*. They were finally married on 8 January 1856 in a chapel so packed that the doors had to be closed half an hour before the service was due to begin. Their married life was touched by sadness, but their love for one another never faltered. They were also partners together in gospel ministry.

Digging deeper

It's very hard for us to appreciate the impact that the arrival of Spurgeon had on London life. As noted in the introduction to this book, the Victorian era was a time when religion was much more central in the life of the British nation than it is today. Newspapers regularly carried reports of church services. A popular preacher could become, in effect, a Victorian celebrity. And, by the end of 1854, Spurgeon was well on the way to becoming the most popular London preacher of them all.

Given this, it is unsurprising that the young Spurgeon struggled with pride. The tinge of arrogance that Susannah Thompson thought she had detected in her first meeting with her future husband was also noticed by others. It comes across in some of his letters, particularly those written to members of his family. Take this as an example, written to an uncle in 1854: 'You have heard that I am now a Londoner, and a little bit of a celebrity. No college could place me in a higher situation. Our place is one of the pinnacles of the denomination.' All of this was factually true. But was this way of writing perhaps a little boastful? Spurgeon himself was aware of the danger, once writing to his father about his fear that he could become his own servant 'instead of the Lord's'.

His old friend Richard Knill, who had prophesied when Spurgeon was a young boy that he would one day preach to multitudes, wrote to grandfather James that he 'prayed much' for Charles. One of his specific requests for the young man was that popularity would not 'puff him up'. It was a good prayer. Young Charles was battling with feelings of self-importance and pride.

But this was a fight where Spurgeon won the victory. Those who knew him as his ministry developed habitually spoke of his humility and lack of pomposity. What was his secret? Richard Knill had prayed that God would keep his young friend 'at the foot of the cross'; Spurgeon came to a place where he recognised his complete and utter dependence on God. His talents, his ministry – all that he had and all he was – were from God from first to last. It was this realisation, above all else, which kept him humble throughout his remarkable life.

An additional factor helping Spurgeon's humility was the suffering he endured. He was plunged into the suffering of others as he ministered during the cholera outbreak of 1854. And he suffered himself. I have already hinted that Spurgeon was prone to depression. He would also experience much physical suffering. All of this had the effect of encouraging Spurgeon to rely on God all the more. The apostle Paul himself was given a 'thorn in [the] flesh' (2 Corinthians 12:7) to 'keep [him] from becoming conceited'.

Spurgeon was well on the way to becoming the most popular London preacher of them all

Three times he prayed for this 'thorn' to be taken away but God responded by saying: 'My grace is sufficient for you' (2 Corinthians 12:9). Sometimes those who are particularly gifted and are used by God in remarkable ways also experience great suffering. Is this God's way of guarding against the danger of pride? Spurgeon in his own suffering certainly discovered that God's grace was sufficient for him, and knew that God's strength was being 'made perfect' in his own weakness.

Engage

Do you struggle with pride? Perhaps you are growing in your Christian life and being used by Him in different ways? Spurgeon spoke from experience when he counselled others to beware of pride and vanity when things were going well. He would counsel us to do the same.

But perhaps you struggle with some other sin? In a very real sense, the remedy that Spurgeon discovered for pride is the remedy for other sins too. This is to focus on Christ and His cross. As we come to Him we receive forgiveness and learn again our complete and utter dependence on Him. May we learn, along with Spurgeon and along with the apostle Paul, that God's grace is sufficient for us.

NEXT PAGE

Illustration of Spurgeon printed in *Vanity Fair*, 10 Dec 1870

NOTE

1 M. Hopkins, *Nonconformity's Romantic Generation* (Carlisle: Paternoster Press, 2004), p.128.

No. 110. _Spurgeon_   **MEN OF THE DAY No. 16.**   Price 6d.

"_No one has succeeded like him in sketching the comic side of repentance and regeneration._"

CHAPTER 5

Triumph and Disaster

UST as it had been at Waterbeach, so it was in London: the chapels Spurgeon preached in were not large enough to contain all who wanted to hear him. Before the end of his first year at New Park Street, the problem of overcrowding had already become acute. Extra people squeezed into already cramped pews and still more filled the aisles and sat on the pulpit steps. With scant regard for issues of health and safety, any available spot was taken. Some Sundays even saw worshippers perched precariously on the windowsills as they waited for the service to begin. But despite packing people in, increasing numbers were still being turned away. Something had to be done.

The popularity of Spurgeon the preacher

Spurgeon's first thought was to enlarge the existing chapel building. The New Park Street members agreed to this, enthusiasm was high and the money was soon raised. But where would the church meet whilst work on the extension was taking place? Spurgeon suggested a radical way forward. They would rent the Exeter Hall, a well-known secular building. This was in the Strand, an important London thoroughfare just north of the Thames. Exeter Hall had been used for Christian services before, but these had always been special meetings – one-offs. Spurgeon's bold proposal was to use the hall for his church's *regular* worship services. The large building could seat at least 4,000 people. Surely even Spurgeon's preaching would not be able to fill such a place, at least not Sunday after Sunday? It was undoubtedly a risky venture – an act of faith. But, amazingly, beginning in the spring of 1855, huge crowds thronged the Strand and pressed into the Exeter Hall for the services. The newspapers reported that the whole street was sometimes blocked and that, as before, many were unable to get in. If you wanted to hear Spurgeon, you were always well advised to arrive early.

But increasing numbers were now getting the opportunity to

experience his preaching. As well as the larger crowds who could now listen to him on a Sunday, there were many opportunities to hear him at other times. Spurgeon the London pastor had continued his Waterbeach practice of taking services in different places midweek. For a period in the mid-1850s he was doing this almost every evening. It was not only London churches he visited; he was willing to travel further afield, preaching in chapels and also in the open air. But even more importantly, from 1855, one of his sermons was published on a weekly basis. Initially called the *New Park Street Pulpit*, this meant that people all over the country could read what others were hearing, see what all the fuss was about and, more to the point, benefit from Spurgeon's thoroughly biblical, down-to-earth, dynamic gospel preaching. Day by day it seemed that interest in this young pulpit sensation grew. Spurgeon was

ABOVE
Spurgeon
preaching at
the Exeter Hall

happy that Christians were being built up and the gospel was being preached to those who were as yet outside the faith. He relied on prayer and on the support of his family and church friends. But he was undoubtedly working too hard. Frequently he was exhausted. Many close to him could not help but feel anxious.

The renovations at New Park Street would clearly be inadequate now. Once again, there were some crucial decisions to make. Spurgeon announced that a completely new chapel would have to be built on a different site, and he set out to raise funds for the new venture. Rumours spread that the new building would be a sort of nonconformist cathedral and seat upwards of 15,000 people. Unsurprisingly the fashionable London press reacted with amazement and distaste. Spurgeon was undeterred, but the pressure and pace of work was beginning to take its toll on him. In a hastily scribbled letter which dates from this period he reviewed the situation as he saw it: 'Friends firm. Enemies alarmed. Devil angry. Sinners saved. Christ exalted. Self not well.' It was a fair summary.

If hiring the Exeter Hall had been radical, Spurgeon's next move broke entirely new ground. He announced plans to rent the music hall in Surrey Gardens, Kennington. It wasn't just the size of this new venue – the recently built music hall had a capacity of 10,000 – it was the *type* of place it was. The massive hall was used for popular concerts and the park had been home to a zoo. This may seem mild to us but for a church to meet in such a location in the Victorian era caused a sensation. Surrey Gardens was a place where, as one commentator put it, 'wild beasts had been exhibited and wilder men had been accustomed to congregate'. To hire such a place for Sunday services was, for some of Spurgeon's members, a step too far. The music hall was 'the devil's house' and therefore their church must not use it! Spurgeon's characteristic response was that he was 'willing to go even into the devil's house to win souls for Christ'. The reaction of the watching public was mixed. Certainly some rejoiced that the gospel would be proclaimed to so many people. But still others, including Christians, felt that if Spurgeon had not overreached himself before, then he had surely done so now. Wasn't he sacrificing Christian principles and good judgment on the altar of ego and popularity? But although there were many different opinions regarding what Spurgeon was doing, most people were agreed on one thing: they were all curious to see what would happen at the first service at the music hall. This was due to be on Sunday evening 19 October 1856.

Sadly, it was to be the scene of what Spurgeon later described as a 'frightful calamity' and the 'most memorable crisis' of his whole life.

The Surrey Gardens music hall disaster

Any concerns about filling the cavernous music hall were quickly dispelled long before the service was due to begin. As Spurgeon approached Surrey Gardens with plenty of time to spare he could see a vast crowd. The road leading to the main entrance of the hall was 'filled up with a solid block of people who were unable to get into the building'. Fortunately it had been arranged for Spurgeon to gain access via a side entrance. But it was only with difficulty, and with the help of friends effectively acting as minders, that the preacher was able to reach the door and force his way in.

Spurgeon felt anxious and faint. As he was often nervous before preaching, it was unsurprising that he felt so now. How many people were actually there? Accurate estimates are impossible but

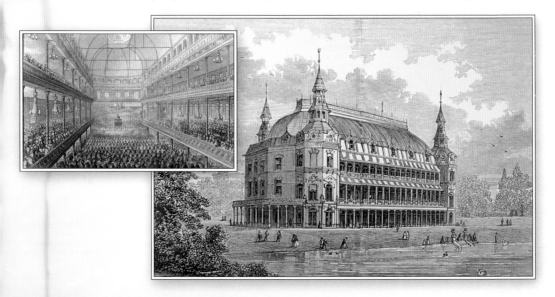

The Times conservative guess was that about 12,000 had somehow managed to cram their way in, with a further 5,000 outside unable to gain admission. Other newspapers put the numbers higher. What is certain is that the building, both at ground level and in the vast overhead galleries, was dangerously full. This was something the preacher could see only too well for himself.

Spurgeon wisely began the service ten minutes early. There was little point waiting as no one else was going to get in anyway. Everything proceeded as normal. There was a prayer, a hymn, a Bible reading, and further prayers, all led by Spurgeon. This was just like a normal church service. Spurgeon had insisted that there was going to be nothing different or flashy about the meeting. The congregation were perhaps a little restive but generally attentive. What happened next is disputed. Some accounts suggest that a group shouted that the galleries were collapsing; others said that the shout had been 'fire'. Certainly there were shouts of alarm. Spurgeon stopped his prayer and looked up. From his vantage point on the platform he could see no evidence of any fire or collapse. Almost certainly the cries were malicious, a deliberate attempt to cause trouble. Spurgeon immediately tried to calm the crowd, but in various parts of the building panic had already set in. People rushed for the exits and part of a staircase leading down from one of the galleries gave way. Those who fell were trampled underfoot and there was a terrible crush, particularly on the stairwell but also elsewhere in the hall. Many were injured, some very seriously. Tragically seven people lost their lives. Those who by their shouts caused the panic were never caught.

As Spurgeon stood on the platform trying to restore order he was unaware of the extent of the disaster. People at the front started shouting out for him to preach and after a brief lull he was persuaded to try. He abandoned his prepared message and tried to speak instead on how the 'terror and alarm' of this evening would be 'as nothing' compared to the coming day of judgment. Spurgeon would later be pilloried in sections of the press, firstly for preaching at all in the circumstances and, secondly, for choosing this theme.

LEFT

Surrey Gardens Music Hall exterior and interior

But Spurgeon still did not know the scale of the tragedy; he was unaware of the collapsed staircase and that there had been any loss of life. Other rumours that surfaced in the newspapers, for example that the deacons passed round collection plates even as attempts were being made to help the dying, were almost certainly false.

Spurgeon's rather stumbling and confused attempt at preaching failed – there was yet more noise and commotion and he felt he could not go on. As he closed the service, he urged people to leave in a calm and orderly way: 'Do not ... be in a hurry. Let those nearest the door go first,' he pleaded. Spurgeon then collapsed and had to be helped from the platform. Only then did he hear that there had been fatalities. He fainted again and was taken away to the house of a friend. Some who saw this thought that the preacher himself had died. There were days immediately after this terrible tragedy when Spurgeon almost wished this were true.

Spurgeon's 'dark night of the soul'

Spurgeon was shielded by friends from the acres of bitter and, frankly, libellous press comment which followed in the aftermath of the disaster. But he was almost completely crushed in spirit. He passed through what he called a 'horror of great darkness'. Day and night he relived the terrible events – the shouts, the panic, the moment he had heard of the deaths; he replayed them in his mind over and over again. Everything was a confused and horrible whirl. He was, he said, incapable of 'mental effort'. Worse still, prayer seemed impossible. God seemed very distant. Even the sight of the Bible brought from him 'a flood of tears'. Spurgeon was experiencing a deep spiritual depression, what spiritual writers of old used to call 'a dark night of the soul'. And for some time there seemed to be no escape.

Mercifully, Spurgeon was delivered from the worst of this. He himself recalled that, a number of days after the catastrophe, all of a sudden 'the name of Jesus flashed through my mind'. At that moment:

> The person of Christ seemed visible to me. I stood still. The burning
> lava of my soul was cooled. My agonies were hushed. I bowed
> myself there, and the garden that had seemed a Gethsemane
> became to me a Paradise.

It was an experience of the risen Christ that reassured Spurgeon of God's love for him. Moreover, he now believed that God still had a plan and purpose for his life. Many had suggested that Spurgeon's ministry was effectively finished. How, they said, could he ever recover? But now Spurgeon felt he had been given the strength and courage to go on.

It is worth pausing here for a moment's reflection, for Spurgeon's experience speaks powerfully to us. If we have felt as Spurgeon did in those dark days immediately after the Surrey Gardens disaster, if we are experiencing a 'dark night of the soul', identifying with Spurgeon in his distress, his loss of hope and his feeling that God had abandoned him, then we can know that, in Christ, God *does* love us. However tough things are, God has a plan and purpose for our lives.

Although Spurgeon recovered, his life remained marked by this disaster. He confessed that he did not think he could have continued his ministry had he been involved in a second, similar, incident. If this had happened he would have had to give up preaching. He was often visibly anxious when taking services in crowded buildings. This was especially so when there were galleries which looked as if they might be unsafe. For the rest of his life he would suffer from what a modern biographer has described as 'periodic attacks of acute depression brought on by the recollection of the Surrey Gardens disaster'.[1] In terms borrowed from *The Pilgrim's Progress*, Spurgeon described these experiences in the following way: 'There are dungeons underneath the Castle of Despair as dreary as the abodes of the lost, and some of us have been in them.' More straightforwardly he told a friend that 'in the lone watches of the night' he sometimes found himself unable to sleep and in dreadful anguish.

However tough things are, God has a plan and purpose for our lives

All of this is a reminder that Spurgeon's story is not just a story of triumph – a journey of serene progress from one success to the next. The road on which he travelled as a pilgrim was one which was marked by suffering as well as joy.

Recovering from the tragedy

Spurgeon's church was stunned by what had happened on the night of the disaster. But they remained loyal to their pastor, and were deeply concerned by his struggles in its immediate aftermath. They gave themselves to prayer. For a while they must have feared for their young minister. But their loyalty and love, their prayers, and Spurgeon's own vivid experience of the risen Christ, all combined to give him the courage to preach again. Amazingly, pastor and people agreed that they should return to the scene of tragedy which had caused Spurgeon such terrible anguish of spirit. On 23 November, Spurgeon stood for a second time in the Surrey Gardens music hall, surveyed the crowd that had gathered, and began to preach.

Whilst they had strongly believed it was right to return to Surrey Gardens, Spurgeon and the church had made an important concession, deciding to hold their service in the morning, not in the evening as before. It was considered that the gathering darkness had been a major factor leading to the panic and crush of the previous month. To everyone's immense relief, this time the service passed off without incident. In fact, Spurgeon would continue to preach at Surrey Gardens until the end of 1859, when the decision of the owners to open the amusement park on a Sunday led him to stop hiring the music hall in protest.

During this time, countless numbers of people had become Christians in what was one of the most fruitful periods of Spurgeon's long ministry. Having left Surrey Gardens in 1859, the congregation returned, briefly, to Exeter Hall. But in March 1861 the new purpose-built chapel was finally opened. This was the Metropolitan Tabernacle in Newington Butts, south London. The church had learnt from their former, disastrous relocation to New Park Street and this time the site had been carefully chosen. The transport links were good and there was none of the heavy industry or potential for flooding which had caused such problems before. For pastor and church, a new era was dawning.

The Metropolitan Tabernacle

They had eventually decided on a building with a seating capacity of 5,000, not the 15,000 that had been rumoured in the press. An echo of the Surrey Gardens tragedy can be seen in the close attention that was given to the emergency exits. Spurgeon was relieved

that, if necessary, the whole building could be safely cleared in five minutes. The final cost of the project was £31,000, an astronomical sum for the time. Donations, large and small, came in from those who had heard Spurgeon speak around the country and who had read his printed sermons. But it was the members and friends of Spurgeon's own church who perhaps gave most sacrificially. There were times when he, the deacons and the building committee were anxious that the money might not be raised. But these fears were not realised. One person alone gave £5,000. By the time the 'Tab' opened, the building had been completely paid for. (The current Metropolitan Tabernacle in London's Elephant and Castle district is not the original building, which was damaged by fire in 1898 and then again by bombing in World War Two. But the imposing frontage is original. Looking at this gives some idea of the scale of the first 'Met Tab'. By any standards it was an impressive structure.)

Of course, there were people who were quick to denounce this as yet another ego trip for Spurgeon, and accuse the church – and especially the pastor – of delusions of grandeur. Spurgeon's response

ABOVE
The Metropolitan Tabernacle, destroyed by fire in 1898
LEFT
The original design for the Metropolitan Tabernacle. Because of the expense, the four towers were never built.

was to say that he could not bear to see people going away disappointed because they could not get in to hear the gospel preached. It was only 'with a view of winning more souls to God' that the Tabernacle was built the size it was. This focus on the gospel was typical of Spurgeon. It was this, together with his experience of God's power and love and the support of his church, which had carried him through what had been such a traumatic period in his life.

I have the privilege of teaching at Spurgeon's College in London. Recently, I was attending a chapel service where the preacher, David Coffey, took the passage Matthew 14:22–33. Here, Jesus walks on water whilst His disciples are battling a furious storm in their boat. When the disciple Peter sees Jesus, he gets out of the boat and steps on to the water himself, walking towards Jesus. But then he takes his eyes off his Lord, and looks instead at the crashing waves and listens to the roaring wind. He is afraid and begins to sink, crying out for help. Jesus reaches out and saves him, and later calms the waves and the wind. David made a number of points as he applied the passage to our lives today. One of these was that Jesus is in the eye of the storm with us and another was that when faith is sinking, Jesus saves. Spurgeon had been in the eye of storm but he had discovered that Jesus was with him. And when his faith had begun to sink, Jesus had reached out and saved him. The message proclaimed in Spurgeon's College chapel, over 150 years after the Surrey Gardens disaster, had in fact been the experience of the college's founder all those years ago. Spurgeon guessed he would have to pass through many more storms in his eventful life. But he knew beyond all doubt that he would not have to face them alone.

ABOVE
The Metropolitan
Tabernacle
RIGHT
Spurgeon
preaching at the
Crystal Palace

🖪 Digging deeper

It's worth reflecting on the fact that, by the end of the events described in this chapter, the former 'boy preacher of the Fens' had become the most popular preacher in the whole of Victorian Britain. What was the secret of Spurgeon's extraordinary success? Was it entirely due to his natural gifts, as some thought, or were other factors at work? To help us consider this we can spend a few moments looking in more depth at perhaps the most extraordinary service Spurgeon ever took. This was on Wednesday 7 October 1857, and so falls within the period we have covered in this chapter.

This particular service was not arranged by Spurgeon or his church. The Wednesday in question had been proclaimed a national fast day – by the government. A special service was to be held. Who was to preach at such an auspicious occasion? The choice fell on Spurgeon. This was an unusual privilege for any nonconformist minister and an extraordinary honour for one so young. And the venue was to be none other than the Crystal Palace, where Charles and Susannah Spurgeon had done their courting! Only a few years previously Charles had sat in the audience following the palace's relocation, just a face in the crowd, watching the grand procession go by. Now all eyes would be on him as he stood to preach.

If the Exeter Hall was large and the Surrey Gardens music hall

vast, the Crystal Palace was on a different scale entirely. It was more than three times the length of St Paul's Cathedral.

Up until this point, it has not been possible to be absolutely certain about the exact numbers coming to hear Spurgeon speak, but here it is different, as admission was through turnstiles which recorded each person entering. By the time all had entered for the service, these turnstiles had clicked a grand total of 23,654 times – the largest congregation to which Spurgeon would ever preach. Some suggest this may still be the largest indoor congregation that has ever gathered to hear a preacher. At the time Spurgeon was just twenty-three years of age.

What would he preach to this huge crowd, which included rows of politicians and nobility? Surely he would soften his message? No. Even here, Spurgeon was determined to proclaim the gospel. He repeatedly explored three great themes in his preaching. The first was the sheer majesty and holiness of God. The second was the utter sinfulness of humankind. The third was the cross of Christ, which bridged the gap between the first and second themes – it was the cross that made it possible for sinful human beings to have a relationship with the glorious God.[2] These were the notes he repeatedly struck in his regular preaching ministry. Here, with the eyes of so many on him, his message was the same. The uncompromising commitment to the gospel should surely be seen as one of the great secrets of his success.

Spurgeon began his message by denouncing sin. He bravely spoke against immorality on the streets of London, factory owners who oppressed their workforces and moneymen who cheated others. In fact, Spurgeon challenged all his listeners that day about sin and judgment and the need for repentance. He then spoke of God as the 'Almighty' and 'Most High', just as earlier in his prayers he had exalted the majesty of the Lord. The Christian God was the Maker of all, before whom all people would one day stand. What, then, could sinners do? How could they stand before a holy God? Was it possible to know His forgiveness? Spurgeon moved to reassure his vast audience. Because of Christ's death for them they could be saved. The Son of God, said Spurgeon, had died 'that we might not die'. Now, to every true believer, 'heaven's gate' was open.

Spurgeon always spoke in the language of the people. He would certainly be sensitive to the audience he was speaking to, and was ready to change his approach to suit the occasion. But he never compromised his essential message in the slightest, as his preaching at the Crystal Palace shows. As he closed the service, surveying the great mass of humanity before him, he declared that he had never set out to court popularity. As God was his witness, he had never sought fame; his aim had always been to please God and speak His truth. Spurgeon wasn't interested in crowds but he was interested in conversions. And, he assured the people, 'if one poor sinner shall look to Jesus ... enough is done, for God is honoured'. Spurgeon's overriding passion was to bring the gospel to those who needed to hear. It was a passion which never changed.

If this was a key reason for Spurgeon's success there was another – the power of God. Once again this is illustrated by his ministry at the Crystal Palace. Spurgeon was concerned that, in such an auditorium, even *his* voice might not be audible in the furthest parts of the building. A day or two before the service a portable pulpit was set up and Spurgeon went to test the acoustics. Standing in the place where he would preach he repeatedly cried out, 'Behold the Lamb of God, which taketh away the sin of the world' (John 1:29, AV). The words from John's Gospel echoed round the building. It seemed that Spurgeon's voice would be up to the task after all.

Unknown to the preacher there was a workman in one of the galleries. This man heard the simple Bible verse being proclaimed and, for him, the words 'came like a message from heaven to his soul'. He put down his tools and went home. After a brief struggle he gave his life to the Lord, finding, as Spurgeon was to later put it, 'peace and life by beholding the Lamb of God'. An incident like this cannot be explained by Spurgeon's speaking ability alone, remarkable as this was. It could only be explained by what we noted in the introduction to this book – God's 'marvellous power'.

... he repeatedly cried out, 'Behold the Lamb of God, which taketh away the sin of the world'

⧉ Engage

How can we sum up the secret of Spurgeon's fruitfulness? The answer has two parts. The first was his faithfulness to the gospel message. Through thick and thin it was the gospel he was determined to preach – nothing more and nothing less. The second part of the answer has to do with the 'marvellous power' of the Holy Spirit. We are called to be faithful to the gospel message, whatever the work is that we are called to do. And as we remain faithful, and as we pray, we can expect to see the 'marvellous power' of God at work, for as we've already noted in this book 'Jesus Christ is the same yesterday and today and for ever' (Hebrews 13:8).

Perhaps we should also note that a fruitful ministry is often one that is marked by suffering. We should not be surprised at this, for we follow a Lord who won His greatest victory on a cross, and who calls us to take up our own cross and follow Him (Mark 8:34). The apostle Paul's ambition was to know Christ and 'the power of his resurrection and the fellowship of sharing in his sufferings' (Philippians 3:10). Spurgeon knew this power – and he also knew what it was like to suffer. But what about us? Can we say that to know Christ's power and to share in His sufferings is *our* ambition?

The events of this chapter have taken us on quite a journey, one of triumph, of disaster, and then triumph again. It might be that you want to reflect on how Jesus really is with *you* in the eye of the storm. It is not only the testimony of Spurgeon, but also of countless other Christians, that when faith is sinking, Jesus does rescue us. As you cry out to Him my prayer is that, just as Spurgeon experienced Jesus' help and deliverance, you would know this too.

NOTES

1   P. Kruppa, *Charles Haddon Spurgeon: A Preacher's Progress* (New York: Garland Publishing, 1982), p.92.

2   Mark Hopkins highlights and explores these themes in his fine study of Spurgeon's theology. See M. Hopkins, *Nonconformity's Romantic Generation*, (Carlisle: Paternoster Press, 2004), pp.140–41; 146.

CHAPTER 6

The Inner Man

The man behind the image

 NE of the aims of this short biography is to get behind the headlines generated by this people's preacher, so we can better appreciate what Spurgeon was *really* like. We have all heard of great preachers who have fallen in their personal lives, or who were very different away from the public gaze. Was Spurgeon like this? Or was he someone who was able to live, by God's grace, with real integrity? That it was a life of service and suffering is beyond doubt. In this chapter, we will start to examine the 'inner man'.

Service ...

The Metropolitan Tabernacle opened on Monday 18 March 1861, appropriately enough with a prayer meeting. Over 1,000 people came. Spurgeon's first words at the Tabernacle would become widely known. He declared:

> 'I would propose that the subject of the ministry in this house ...
> shall be the person of JESUS CHRIST. I am never ashamed to avow
> myself a Calvinist; I do not hesitate to take the name of Baptist; but
> if I am asked what is my creed, I reply, "It is Jesus Christ."'

He went on to say that Jesus was 'the sum and substance of the gospel' and the 'incarnation of every precious truth'. It was a great beginning. Spurgeon's overriding commitment to Christ was an inspiration to those around him. It remains an inspiration for us today.

The first full services at the Tabernacle were on 29 March and 31 March – Good Friday and Easter Sunday in 1861. Spurgeon immediately started to make good his promise to focus on Christ. On Good Friday he preached twice, and in both messages he concentrated on the Lord Jesus and His cross. On Easter Sunday the church met at the Tabernacle in the evening to praise the risen Christ. During the course of the service Spurgeon uttered the following words:

> 'Let God send the fire of His Spirit here, and the minister will be more and more lost in his Master. You will come to think less of the speaker and more of the truth spoken; the individual will be swamped, the words uttered will rise above everything.'

Aware of the cult of personality, Spurgeon wanted all to know that he was a servant of Christ, and that his desire was to preach Christ's gospel in the power of the Holy Spirit.

As regular ministry at the Tabernacle got underway, there were many who were watching to see how things would develop. There were those who, even now, were expecting (and perhaps hoping) that the crowds would grow tired of Spurgeon and his message. But, as ever, they were to be disappointed. Each Sunday, morning and evening, the great building was filled with people who came to worship God and hear His Word preached. Cabbies would drive their horse-drawn hansom cabs around the streets of north London every Sunday, hoping to pick up fares with their shout of 'over the water to Charlie'. It was a practice which had started in Spurgeon's New Park Street days and then, as now, the canny cab drivers did good business! People came from all over the city, and beyond, to the Tabernacle services.

It would be easy to get the impression that the Tabernacle was just a preaching centre. Probably this was true to an extent. Some people did come because they loved hearing Spurgeon and were attracted by his celebrity. They were 'sermon tasters', but they never made a real commitment to the church. Even some who became members of the Tabernacle were probably little involved beyond attendance on a Sunday. But this was never Spurgeon's intention. When people asked to join the 'Tab', he did his best to interview each applicant himself. This was not only to satisfy himself that the prospective member was truly a Christian. Spurgeon also wanted to impress on them the importance of the regular prayer meetings and of active Christian service. He did not want anyone to become a member who did 'not promise beforehand to undertake, if at all possible, some useful work for the benefit of others'. During Spurgeon's pastorate at the Tabernacle, people came into membership at an average of more than one a day. Many of these had been converted under Spurgeon's preaching. And a good number of them fulfilled their promise to their pastor to give themselves to 'useful work'. The wider ministry of the church was extremely dynamic and exciting.

... and suffering

However, at the same time, a thread of suffering continued to run through Spurgeon's life. The depression Spurgeon had experienced in the aftermath of the Surrey Gardens disaster periodically returned, although not with quite the same intensity. Nevertheless, there were still dark times in Spurgeon's life, and these periods of depression were now accompanied by deteriorating physical health. As the 1860s wore on Spurgeon suffered increasingly from what was then known as Bright's disease – chronic kidney infection. And, from about 1867, he was also inflicted with rheumatic gout. At times Spurgeon was in agony – it was almost too much to bear. If the pain struck at night he would be quite unable to sleep. Sometimes he would ask Susannah to read to him, and this brought him some comfort. But often he would just silently cry out to his Lord. In this way Spurgeon learnt to find God in the midst of his distress. In fact he would testify that some of his closest times with his Lord were when he was in this state. His suffering also gave him great empathy with people who were going through difficulties of their own – those of his hearers who were coping with, say, illness or bereavement, or who were just struggling with the harshness of life in the grime and grind of Victorian London. Such people felt that here was a preacher who somehow understood what they themselves were going through. Many commented on Spurgeon's compassion and his 'pastor's heart'. But often they were not fully aware of the personal suffering which helped him to have such sympathy with others who struggled in different ways.

The real man?

... a great ocean steamer, powered by a mighty engine ...

So far on our journey to discover the real man, we have uncovered some of the influences by which Spurgeon was shaped for a lifetime's service, and we have seen, by looking at his preaching, how his fruitfulness flowed from gospel faithfulness and dependence on the power of the Holy Spirit. His life was also shot through with a vein of suffering, as we have seen in reading about the Surrey Gardens disaster, and his depression and illnesses. But if we are *truly* going to uncover the real man, we need to go deeper still and tackle questions about his devotional life and personal holiness – starting with prayer and the Bible.

no prayer, no power!

Spurgeon and prayer

We read at the start of this chapter of a prayer meeting at the Tabernacle, and we have also seen something of Spurgeon's own private prayer life – crying out to the Lord in distress during the night. It's almost impossible to write Spurgeon's story without referring often to prayer, because it was so central for him.

Spurgeon always delighted to meet with other Christians to pray. He compared the Tabernacle to a great ocean steamer, powered by a mighty engine. That engine was the various weekly prayer meetings which were central in the church's life. Without these Spurgeon believed that 'the ship' would quickly come to a halt – no prayer, no power! In these meetings, most of the time was given over to intercession – prayers for the work of the church and the

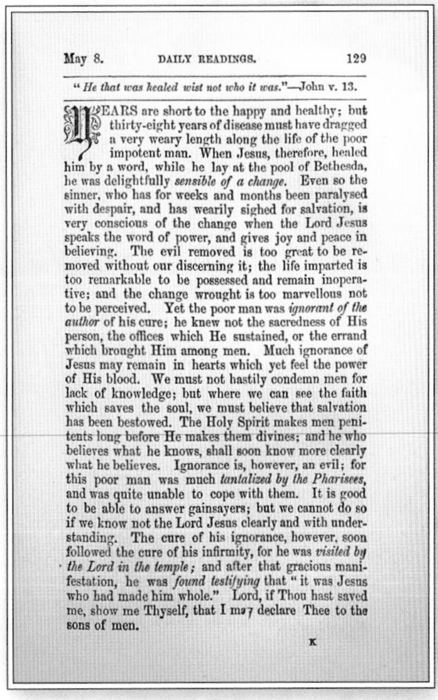

May 8. DAILY READINGS. 129

"*He that was healed wist not who it was.*"—John v. 13.

YEARS are short to the happy and healthy; but thirty-eight years of disease must have dragged a very weary length along the life of the poor impotent man. When Jesus, therefore, healed him by a word, while he lay at the pool of Bethesda, he was delightfully *sensible of a change.* Even so the sinner, who has for weeks and months been paralysed with despair, and has wearily sighed for salvation, is very conscious of the change when the Lord Jesus speaks the word of power, and gives joy and peace in believing. The evil removed is too great to be removed without our discerning it; the life imparted is too remarkable to be possessed and remain inoperative; and the change wrought is too marvellous not to be perceived. Yet the poor man was *ignorant of the author* of his cure; he knew not the sacredness of His person, the offices which He sustained, or the errand which brought Him among men. Much ignorance of Jesus may remain in hearts which yet feel the power of His blood. We must not hastily condemn men for lack of knowledge; but where we can see the faith which saves the soul, we must believe that salvation has been bestowed. The Holy Spirit makes men penitents long before He makes them divines; and he who believes what he knows, shall soon know more clearly what he believes. Ignorance is, however, an evil; for this poor man was much *tantalized by the Pharisees,* and was quite unable to cope with them. It is good to be able to answer gainsayers; but we cannot do so if we know not the Lord Jesus clearly and with understanding. The cure of his ignorance, however, soon followed the cure of his infirmity, for he was *visited by the Lord in the temple;* and after that gracious manifestation, he was *found testifying* that "it was Jesus who had made him whole." Lord, if Thou hast saved me, show me Thyself, that I may declare Thee to the sons of men.

K

ABOVE
A page from his book *Morning by Morning*

progress of God's kingdom in the wider world – although there was always opportunity for praise and thanksgiving as well. They were well attended: the Monday night meeting continued to draw about 1,000 people on a regular basis. Spurgeon lamented the fact that more did not come!

Spurgeon invited different people to lead in prayer at the meetings – it wasn't just he himself who prayed. He had characteristically strong views about the way people should pray. He made clear his disapproval of long rambling petitions: 'strength not length' was one of his maxims. Those who sought to show off, deliberately using fine-sounding words and displaying their mastery of difficult doctrines, also provoked Spurgeon's displeasure. Most importantly, spoken prayers which were cold, formal and did not flow from the heart were worse than useless. On the other hand, it didn't matter to Spurgeon if someone stumbled over their words or became tongue-tied. In summary, short prayers that were full of faith and 'real' were what he was after. And did God answer their many requests? Spurgeon was sure that He did – again and again. However turbulent the waters through which they passed, the engine of prayer kept the great ship of the Tabernacle moving forward.

Spurgeon's own personal prayer life was remarkable. His basic pattern was to pray morning and evening, as the title of his famous book of daily readings suggests.[1] Sometimes he would pray with his family (his twin sons, Thomas and Charles, were born on 20 September 1856); sometimes he would be alone. But his prayer life certainly did not stop there; Spurgeon wanted to maintain continued communion with God throughout the day. One of the ways he sought to do this was by praying short, one-sentence prayers as he went about his daily work. Friends spoke of seeing him pray as he wrote a letter, as he was reading a book, or whilst he was out walking. Speaking of his own experiences, he said: 'Some of us could honestly say that we are seldom a quarter of an hour without speaking to God.' These short, pithy prayers are what have sometimes been called 'arrow prayers', prayers addressed to God in the midst of a day full of all sorts of different tasks. They were a vital part of Spurgeon's devotional life.

Spurgeon also believed in setting aside longer periods for prayer and reflection, seeking to spend quality time with God. These occasions would include much spoken prayer – praise, confession, thanksgiving and intercession. But they would also include space for quiet and contemplation. He once said, 'I like sometimes in prayer, when I do not feel I can say anything, just to sit still, and look up.' When he did this, in 'solemn silence', Spurgeon experienced fellowship with Jesus 'of a closer sort than words could possibly express'. These times of uninterrupted prayer and contemplation were extremely important to Spurgeon and led to growing intimacy with Jesus. It is clear that he was sustained, in life and in ministry, through prayer.

Spurgeon and the Bible

The Scriptures were vitally important to Spurgeon. He was committed to the Bible as God's trustworthy Word; he preached from the Bible as faithfully as he could; he loved the Bible because of the way it revealed Jesus to him. Famously, he refused to mount a detailed intellectual defence of the Scriptures when their authority was under attack from various nineteenth-century critics. Defend the Bible? For Spurgeon one might as well talk of defending a lion; it wasn't necessary! Rather, Christians should be 'letting the lion loose' to do his work of convicting and converting the world. When the Bible was applied to people's hearts by the Holy Spirit, then they would know its truth and feel its power.

As far as his own life was concerned, Spurgeon was clear that the lion of the Scriptures would be free to do whatever it wanted.

He was determined to live a life that was shaped by God's Word. Once, when preaching, he gave moving testimony as to how God had dealt with him through the Bible, which he referred to simply as 'the Book'. He declared:

'[T]he Book has wrestled with me; the Book has smitten me; the Book has comforted me; the Book has smiled on me; the Book has frowned on me; the Book has clasped my hand; the Book has warmed my heart. The Book weeps with me, and sings with me, it whispers to me; and it preaches to me; it maps my way, and holds up my goings; it was to me the "Young Man's Companion", and it is still my "Morning and Evening" chaplain. It is a live Book: all over alive; from its first chapter to its last word it is full of a strange mystic vitality, which makes it have pre-eminence over every other writing for every living child of God.'

These urgent words show that, for Spurgeon, the Bible was a vibrant, living book. It was fresh, vital, always relevant and absolutely crucial to his ongoing walk with God.

Given this, it's not surprising that Spurgeon spent much time reading and meditating on the Scriptures. Morning and evening he would not only pray, but also read God's Word. He would, as well, meditate on different verses during the day and he would study the Bible for his preaching and writing. As yet we've not thought much about Spurgeon's writing ministry, but he produced many valuable books. Probably the writing project he gave most time to was the multi-volume *Treasury of David*, a massive commentary on the Psalms. Completing this was, for Spurgeon, a labour of love. Despite its size, and the great learning it contained, it was a million miles away from being dry, dusty or dull. Rather it was full of warm and inspiring Bible exposition, with much practical teaching carefully applied to the lives of believers. Commenting on the longest of all the Psalms, Psalm 119, Spurgeon noted that this spoke of the 'fullness, certainty, clearness, and sweetness of the Word of God'. Those who understood the psalm would come to see that whole of

... he loved the Bible because of the way it revealed Jesus to him

Scripture was like a brilliant, beautiful island made entirely of pearl. This was Spurgeon's own experience which he wanted his readers to share. The whole of the Bible was in fact a treasury to him. Just as he felt he could not carry on without prayer; so he believed he could not live without the Scriptures.

✝ Digging deeper

It is obvious that prayer and the Bible were central for Spurgeon. Most importantly, it was through prayer and reading the Scriptures that he grew in intimacy with God. And it was Spurgeon's deep knowledge of the one true God – Father, Son and Holy Spirit – from which all his activity in the church and in the wider world sprang. This dynamic inter-relationship, between *intimacy* with God on the one hand, and *involvement* in Christian service on the other, is evident in a prayer Spurgeon prayed in one of the Tabernacle services. In heartfelt, emotional language, Spurgeon prayed:

Oh to love the Saviour with a passion that can never cool … Oh to delight in God with a holy overflowing rejoicing that can never be stopped, so that we might live to glorify God at the highest bent of our powers, living with enthusiasm, burning, blazing, being consumed with the indwelling God who worketh all things in us according to His will.

Do you see the relationship between intimacy and involvement worked out in this passionate prayer? Spurgeon's heart's desire was to increasingly delight in God. He wanted to know Him more, to love Him more, to enjoy closer and closer fellowship with Him. But his longing did not stop there. Out of this deepening personal knowledge he wanted to 'live to glorify God' with energy and 'enthusiasm'. Different writers on Christian spirituality have noted the incredible energy that flows from a truly contemplative life. Spurgeon is a shining example of this important principle. May God grant that there would be many more in our own day and generation.

Engage

Every aspect of Spurgeon's approach to prayer and the Bible challenges us. Just one thing we could learn is the importance of giving *time* to prayer and the Scriptures. As to Bible reading, Spurgeon was sure that many people of his own day approached the Scriptures too casually and read too quickly. They never grasped the message of the particular verse or passage they were looking at, and never lingered long enough for God to truly speak with them. Such an approach was little more than a 'mechanical exercise' devoid of what Spurgeon called the 'soul of reading'. By contrast he advocated that the reader, having prayed earnestly for the help of the Holy Spirit, read slowly and meditatively. He chided his hearers:

> Do not many of you read the Bible in a hurried way – just a little bit and off you go? Do you not soon forget what you have read, and lose what little effect it seemed to have? How few of you are resolved to get to its soul, its juice, its life, its essence, and to drink in its meaning?

If this was what Spurgeon said to his nineteenth-century hearers, what would he say to people today? More to the point, what would

LEFT
Statue of Spurgeon
at Spurgeon's
College, South
Norwood

he say to you and me?

But perhaps the central lesson is this: one of involvement *flowing out* of intimacy. In my work as a pastor I have met people who are involved up to the hilt in Christian service, but whose work does not flow out of a deep, personal spirituality. There is a real danger they will experience burnout in their lives or, if this does not happen, that their service will become a habit and a chore, not driven by a passion for God and compassion for people. Spurgeon declared that: 'If our life is all in public, it will be a frothy, vapoury, ineffectual existence; but if we hold high converse with God in secret, we shall be mighty for good.' May we all follow Spurgeon's example and grow in intimacy with God. Then we will also be able to glorify Him in our daily lives.

NOTE

1 C.H. Spurgeon, *Morning and Evening*. This was originally published as two separate little books, *Morning by Morning* and *Evening by Evening*. It is available in a number of modern editions; See, for example, the lovely new edition, C.H. Spurgeon, *Morning and Evening* (Fearn, Scotland: Christian Focus, 2007). It can also be found on the internet (http://www.ccel.org/ccel/spurgeon/morneve/).

CHAPTER 7

A Passion for Holiness

UST as Spurgeon spoke much about prayer and Bible reading, so he had much to say about the importance of personal holiness. It was absolutely imperative, he said, that all believers should seek to lead holy lives. This was a theme which featured strongly throughout his ministry. This was true not only of his preaching, but also of his writing and his public prayers.

As far as his preaching was concerned, Spurgeon once boldly declared that 'whenever Jesus Christ draws near to a soul, he comes ... to make it clean'. His vision of the Christian life was one where God continually purified and refined His people. They themselves should desire holiness with a 'spiritual intensity'. As to his writing, in the *Treasury of David* he called the pursuit of holiness a 'noble ambition' and a 'glorious enterprise'. Some people maintained that holy people were basically miserable. But Spurgeon wrote that holiness and happiness were closely linked. The truly holy person would be full of deep and lasting joy. All in all, it was his 'life's ambition', he said, to be holy.

But it was perhaps in his prayers that Spurgeon's passion for holiness was given its freest rein. On one occasion he prayed: 'O Lord, our God, we have an intense desire to be rid of sin. We long after holiness.' On another:

'We do not fight with the powers of darkness as we ought ... yet there *is* something within us which pants after holiness. The divine spark which we have within us cannot be content till it has burned up sin. Thou hast been pleased to quicken us by Thy grace, and to make us Thy children; and nothing ever will content our spirits until we are wholly given up to Thy service.'

Spurgeon rarely missed an opportunity to commend pure, holy, Christlike living. Those who experienced his ministry must have been very clear about the importance he attached to it.

This whole chapter could have been filled up with quotations like these from Spurgeon's preaching, books or prayers. This would have been no bad thing, for his words are nearly always challenging and inspirational. Spurgeon is never dull, and his recorded words are full of powerful, meaty instruction, together with tremendous zeal for Christ and His cause. Spurgeon has much to teach us today, not only on the value of personal holiness, but on a whole host of other subjects, too. But we need to remember that our focus is on whether Spurgeon's *life* actually matched his *words*. As to prayer and Bible reading, this was certainly the case. But what about holiness? Did Spurgeon actually practise what he preached? Or did his public pronouncements mask serious private flaws which he failed to address and which were kept hidden from others?

Financial integrity

The first point to make is that Spurgeon was a man of great financial integrity. This is important because he could have become extremely wealthy. He was pastor of the largest Baptist church, in terms of membership and attendance, in the whole world. And his printed sermons, pamphlets and books were sold in increasing numbers both in Britain and around the globe. In 1871, the number of printed sermons sold weekly in Britain was regularly topping 25,000. And in 1879 the number of sermons sold in total in America reached 500,000. There were rumours that Spurgeon was feathering his own nest and that the pastor of the Metropolitan Tabernacle was a very rich man. But the reality was somewhat different.

One way of showing this is to refer to an event that happened in 1879, although this is to jump ahead a little in our story. This year was the twenty-fifth anniversary of Spurgeon's coming to London, and his church was keen to mark this auspicious occasion, calling it a pastoral silver wedding! At a special event which was organised in Spurgeon's honour, a key deacon, William Olney, was due to be one of the speakers. Olney decided to take the opportunity to put the record straight about their pastor's attitude to money. Speaking with insider knowledge, Olney reckoned that Spurgeon had set the church an 'example of giving' throughout his ministry. Olney revealed what he probably should have kept secret, that Spurgeon had personally contributed almost £5,000 to the Tabernacle building fund. And now the building was up and running, Spurgeon paid for all the cleaning and lighting himself! Olney spoke warmly of his pastor's self-denial and open-hearted generosity. And he had plenty of facts at his disposal to back up what he said.

At the close of his short address, Olney announced that money had been collected from congregation members and other well-wishers so that Spurgeon could be given a special gift for his 'silver jubilee'. The amount raised was £6,233! Spurgeon, who had known about the collection, had already indicated what he would do once this was presented to him. 'Not one farthing for me ... I will not keep it. It shall all be the Lord's, and all shall belong to the Lord's cause.' When Spurgeon rose to reply to Olney's speech, he spoke of his longing to do 'more for the cause of Christ, and more for the poor'. He continued:

> 'The outside world cannot understand that a man should be moved by any motive except that of personal gain; but, if they knew the power of love to Jesus, they would understand that, to the lover of the Saviour, greed of wealth is as vile as the dust beneath his feet.'

Spurgeon was as good as his word, and the whole collection was given away. Spurgeon was scrupulously honest with money, as well as being incredibly generous. The Spurgeons' financial integrity reminds one of Billy and Ruth Graham from a later generation. The example of these couples is a challenge to all Christian leaders today.

Family life

Family life is a further indicator of holiness. All too often a family know a different, and less attractive, side to a person's character

Spurgeon was scrupulously honest with money, as well as being incredibly generous

than that seen even by close friends. How someone behaves in the home is a vital test of true holiness. How does Spurgeon measure up in this regard? The answer is: extremely well.

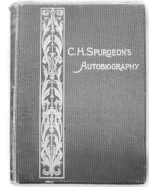

Charles and Susannah's marriage was a very happy one, but they also had to face personal heartbreak. Their twin sons, Thomas and Charles, brought much joy. But Susannah and Charles were unable to have any more children and, from the time of the twins' birth onward, Susannah was often unwell.

But despite (or maybe in part because of) these trials, the Spurgeons' love for one another, which had been strong at the very beginning, grew year by year. 'Susie', according to her husband, was his 'angel of delight'. Susannah unstintingly supported Charles in all his work to the very end. She was involved in the life of the Tabernacle in various ways. For example, she supervised a book fund which provided commentaries and other helpful works for pastors who did not have ready access to such books. The warmth and tenderness of her love for Charles can be gauged from various comments included in the *Autobiography*.[1] Writing a few years after her husband's death, and reminiscing on

their married life together, she said he had been a man of 'sweet humility' and 'gentle kindness'. Moreover, he had a 'mighty faith in God' and had lived a 'glorious and blameless' life. As she wrote these words she was looking at a portrait of Charles as a young man, and she was moved to tears. Some of the great preachers of this era did not have happy marriages, something for which they themselves were often to blame. But this was not the case with Charles and Susannah Spurgeon.

What about their sons, Thomas and Charles? Were they perhaps neglected children of the manse, who grew up to resent their father's absences and the time he gave to the church? All the evidence tells us that 'Tommy' and 'Charlie' loved their father. This was true when they were young and also when they had reached adulthood and left the family home. Their father's character, said Charles junior, was 'noble and godly'. Tellingly, he said that the 'matchless grace and goodness' his father displayed in public was also 'manifested in the home'. To their parents' immense delight, both boys made clear commitments to Christ and were baptised at the Tabernacle. With no less delight, Charles and Susannah saw both the twins become pastors. Charles Junior ministered at Greenwich, Thomas for a while in the South Pacific. In 1894 Thomas accepted a call to follow his father as pastor of the Metropolitan Tabernacle itself. The pastorate was not entirely successful. It can't have been easy to have followed in the footsteps of Charles Haddon Spurgeon! But nothing would change either boy's estimate of the father. He had always been their kind, wise and 'sturdy' friend.

Love, compassion and friendship

Spurgeon's love and compassion was noticed by many other people. Some time after Spurgeon's death, his friend and biographer, William Young Fullerton, wrote the following:

> Many a five-pound note was sent to his correspondents when they sought his help in need … He knew the value of money and was not careless in the spending of it, but there was not a streak of meanness in his nature: he gave with both hands to those in need.[2]

For Fullerton, Spurgeon was someone who displayed complete 'transparency of character'. He was 'commanding', 'simple' (in the sense of straightforward) and 'selfless'. Most of all he was 'entirely Christ's man'. Fullerton's estimate of Spurgeon can be seen in the words he chose to end his biography. As he reflected on Spurgeon's achievements and, most of all, his character, Fullerton simply said: 'Proudly I stand at the salute!'

TOP LEFT
C.H. Spurgeon's *Autobiography*
BOTTOM LEFT
Spurgeon and his two sons

Fullerton had been very close to Spurgeon and (it could be argued) might be biased in favour of the man who had been his friend and mentor. William Robertson Nicoll was a Christian newspaper editor who had known Spurgeon less well. But Robertson Nicoll's tribute was no less fulsome:

> [Spurgeon] was self-controlled, observant and wise, and he had a homely shrewdness and humour which were very refreshing ... The growth of the Kingdom of grace was his prosperity; the opening of a new vein of spiritual life his wealth ... This spirituality is so rare in men of great powers that it is invariably the way to influence.

Others commented on Spurgeon's 'spirituality': his warm, vital, practical godliness. Perhaps this is the greatest tribute to his personal character. We ought also to note that those who knew Spurgeon best tended not to think of him as primarily Spurgeon the church leader, or Spurgeon the writer, or even Spurgeon the preacher. They thought of him, first and foremost, as Spurgeon the loving and wise friend.

... he smoked cigars to the 'glory of God'!

Spurgeon's faults

Of course, Spurgeon did have faults. First of all, he could be scathing about those he disagreed with in the wider Church. His views on Roman Catholics and the so-called 'High Church Party' in the Church of England, who advocated more ritual in worship, could be colourful, to say the least. Even friends felt that he could, at times, be too severe on opponents. Spurgeon never changed his essential views, but he did regret he had not been more generous. In 1891 he said: 'During the past year I have come to see that there is more love and unity among God's people than is generally believed ... different modes of external worship are as furrows of a field; the field is none the less one.'

Another flaw was that there were periods of his life when he was too busy. He didn't always keep a proper day off and did too much. It's important to work hard and give ourselves to the work God has given us to do. But surely burning the candle at both ends, day in, day out, is not actually honouring to God? To highlight another issue, Spurgeon was a smoker. Spurgeon once said he smoked cigars to the 'glory of God'! Many of us today would certainly count this as a fault. Of course, there wasn't a great understanding in the Victorian era of the harm smoking could do, not only to the smoker but also to others around them.

It should be clear enough that Spurgeon was not perfect, but he was able to address issues in his life by the power of the Holy Spirit. He made some progress in finding a better work–life balance. From 1871 he was able to take a long annual winter break and he also took time off in the summer, usually spending some weeks in Scotland. Spurgeon's preaching at Rothesay, in the Firth of Clyde, the story with which this book began, actually took place when he was on holiday. Certainly this wouldn't have been the most relaxing of days for him! But for most of these holiday weeks he was able to live at a much slower pace. Spurgeon learned that he did need to take time to recharge – physically, mentally and spiritually.

We have already noted that Spurgeon, in his early years, had a real struggle with pride. He wrote in a letter, dated 23 March 1855, that: 'My pride is so infernal that there is not a man on earth who can hold it in, and all their silly attempts are futile; but, then, my Master can do it, and He will.' Spurgeon confessed this, and other struggles, to God on a daily basis. And, although he did not believe that any Christian became perfect in this life, he was able to press on in the life of holiness. Year by year God was developing his character, helping him to overcome some of the defects we've mentioned. As far as pride was concerned, that help bore marvellous fruit. Both William Young Fullerton and Thomas Spurgeon were at pains to highlight a particular quality they found in the Charles Haddon Spurgeon they knew. It was humility. By God's grace, he had been enabled to grow so that an area of weakness became a real strength. By that same grace you and I can grow in the life of holiness, too.

🔖 Digging deeper

We've seen that Spurgeon really was a man of character and integrity. It is worth asking how he reached that level of holiness. What was his approach? A number of things can be said. First of all, we should be clear that Spurgeon depended entirely on the work of the Holy Spirit. He taught that when someone made a commitment to Christ as Saviour and Lord, the Holy Spirit came to dwell in their heart. Through the Spirit the new Christian disciple had power to begin to change and to live differently. On this power they would continue to depend for the whole of their lives. Holiness was a work of God in a believer's life – from beginning to end.

But this did not mean that the Christian just sat back and did nothing; that holiness just happened. Some were teaching that all Christians needed to do was 'let go and let God'. If only they did this, then they would automatically reach a new level of holiness. Spurgeon's view was different. According to him, Christians were 'active agents' in their own sanctification, co-operating with the Holy Spirit in His purifying work. Believers were to pray, read God's Word and then struggle with all God's energy to live out the Bible's teaching (see Colossians 1:29). Only in this way would a Christian make progress in holy living. 'Depend upon it,' Spurgeon declared, 'you and I do not grow holy by going to sleep.' Christians were in a battle – against sin, the world and the devil. And that battle needed to be fought daily. This was Spurgeon's own experience and it was how he encouraged his hearers and readers to think and act.

To sum up, we can draw from a sermon Spurgeon preached on 2 Corinthians 7:1 and the words 'let us cleanse ourselves'. In the course of his message, the preacher declared that Christ dwelt in all of His people, by the Holy Spirit. He worked holiness in the lives of each disciple. But the indwelling Spirit did this by making believers active in their own sanctification. God, declared Spurgeon, 'works it in; you work it out; you have to work out in the outward life what He works in in the inner springs of your spiritual being'.

⊞ Engage

Spurgeon once said: 'Write my life across the sky. I have nothing to conceal.' It is an extraordinary statement. Which one of us could say the same thing? Spend some time in confession before God, and ask Him for the strength and vision to live a holy life. I firmly believe that it's not so much great gifts that God blesses, as great likeness to Christ. True holiness is a vital need for the Church today.

But how do we become holy? Spurgeon's teaching on holiness is, I believe, the teaching of the Bible, and it speaks to us today. We certainly need to pray for God to work holiness in us. But we also need to work this out in our lives, struggling with all the energy God gives us. Are you doing this daily? Spurgeon's teaching on this vital subject calls us to prayer *and* action.

What will this holiness look like? The example of Spurgeon helps point the way. We see that a holy life will be one of integrity and purity. A holy person will be different from the world around them, just as Spurgeon was and, much more importantly, as Jesus was. This will make us vulnerable to ridicule. For many years Spurgeon was pilloried in the press, and Jesus of course suffered ridicule and much worse. We shouldn't be afraid of this but, with the apostle Paul, be ready to suffer for the sake of Christ (see 2 Corinthians 6:4–5).

But a holy person will also be loving and compassionate – they will not be harsh, strident or difficult

'Write my life across the sky. I have nothing to conceal'

(see 2 Corinthians 6:6). Finally, Spurgeon shows us that a holy life is also a joyful life. Holy people are not miserable and sour-faced! Rather they live life to the full, following their Lord Jesus wherever He leads. Thought of this way, the holy life suddenly seems very attractive, which is as it should be. Truly, God calls each one of us to have a passion for holiness.

NOTES

1 This was compiled after Spurgeon's death. Although it mostly contains Charles's own writing, a significant part of it was written by Susannah, including the passage I am quoting from.

2 W.Y. Fullerton, *C.H. Spurgeon: A Biography* (London: Williams and Norgate, 1920).

CHAPTER 8

Wider Ministry and Writing

N THE summer of 1881 an American tourist was visiting London. High on his 'to do' list was a trip to the Metropolitan Tabernacle to hear Spurgeon preach. Later he would write about his experiences in a newspaper article which was entitled 'A Day With Spurgeon'.[1] The man, who only signed himself 'SSP', wrote a detailed and vivid account. Looking at this helps us appreciate what we might call an ordinary Tabernacle service, although in reality there was very little that was ordinary about it.

'A Day With Spurgeon'

Early on the Sunday morning of 21 August, SSP and two friends took the bus through the winding London streets to Newington Butts. As they arrived at the Elephant and Castle, the visitors asked the bus conductor the way to the 'Tab', only to be told not to worry. All they needed to do was 'follow the crowd'. Numbers coming to hear Spurgeon were as high as ever.

They reached the building half an hour early but there were already 'solid columns' of people 'streaming in'. The crowds were watched over by 'two or three policemen', but there was no disorder. The team of stewards were welcoming and helpful, making it clear that they often had Americans coming to the services. A place was found where the three friends were able to sit together, but if they had been any later they might have been disappointed. By the time the service began all seating space had been taken and there were upwards of 500 people standing.

The tourists found themselves sitting in a pew with a 'pleasant faced lady' who was a member of the Tabernacle. The woman had nothing but praise for her pastor. Spurgeon was, she said, the 'most devoted unselfish man in the world, always going about doing good'. Reminiscing, the woman remembered the celebration of Spurgeon's twenty-five years of ministry in London. She spoke in admiration of the way Spurgeon had given all the money presented to him on that occasion 'to the poor'. The woman continued: 'He says he has enough for the present, and the Lord whom he serves will see he does not come to want in the future, unless it is that he should. There never was such a man.' Spurgeon was clearly held in the highest regard. Just before 11.00am 'a short, compact, wholesome looking Englishman ... walked briskly down the aisle to the little platform'. The visitor recognised Spurgeon instantly from the many photographs and drawings he had seen. The buzz of conversation died away. The service was about to start.

Worship began with a hymn which the congregation stood to sing. The Americans were used to an organ and a choir, but the Tabernacle had neither of these (Spurgeon, only half joking, used to call the organ the 'devil's whistle'!). There were no musical instruments at all and the only help the congregation had was that of a precentor. This was a man who stood at the front and helped pitch the first note. But at the right moment the thousands of voices joined together in praise, creating an 'avalanche of sound', which SSP also judged very tuneful. According to the relevant pages in the *Metropolitan Tabernacle Pulpit*, they sang number 913 in the chapel hymn book. This was an eighteenth-century hymn, little known today, which began with the words 'Awake, our drowsy souls'.[2] By the time the five verses had been sung, it's likely that any slumbering souls had indeed been shaken wide awake.

The pattern of the service was fairly standard for the time. Spurgeon led everything himself. There were prayers, both of praise and intercession, and a further hymn. There was also a Bible reading which Spurgeon, as was his custom, interspersed with a running commentary on the passage. This was to help explain some of the more difficult verses and apply them to people's lives. Taken as whole, the worship was both simple and Bible-based.

ABOVE
Spurgeon's personal copy of the Metropolitan Tabernacle hymn book

The American visitor was struck by two things in particular. The first of these was Spurgeon's voice, which was amazingly clear and powerful. The Americans were in the balcony, some distance from the preacher, and they could still hear every word. But Spurgeon was not shouting: in fact, he didn't seem to be straining his voice at all. His delivery was perfectly natural, full of variety and what the visitor called 'sweet unction'. Nearly everyone who ever heard Spurgeon made similar comments. He always seemed to be able to make himself heard at the furthest end of the largest building, and his voice had an expressive, almost musical quality about it. Secondly, for SSP, Spurgeon's prayers stood out. They were described as 'simple', 'earnest' and 'fervent'. As he prayed, Spurgeon seemed to be carrying the vast congregation with him so that, although only one person was speaking, the whole church was silently saying the words along with him. Spurgeon was giving voice to the people's own devotion and requests. Once again, the visitor was highlighting an aspect of Spurgeon's ministry that others regularly commented on. D.L. Moody, the evangelist, thought Spurgeon's public prayers were even more remarkable than his preaching. These prayers could be highly eloquent, but there was no artificial striving after effect. When Spurgeon prayed people felt he was in touch with the living God and they were drawn to pray along with him.

'let us ... cast off the works of darkness, and ... put on the armour of light'

Then, after these prayers, readings and hymns came the time for the sermon. Spurgeon preached, according to the visitor's report, for just under an hour. If this was true, it was slightly longer than normal, as forty to forty-five minutes was standard for most of his Tabernacle messages. The sermon was on Romans 13:11–14. These are verses which include the words 'let us ... cast off the works of darkness, and ... put on the armour of light' (AV). The message can be found in Volume 27 of the *Metropolitan Tabernacle Pulpit*, where it is sermon number 1,614. Spurgeon issued a clarion call to put off the old and put on the new (see Colossians 3:1–14). He focused strongly on the need for purity and, especially, Christlikeness. As the message unfolded he put special emphasis on the phrase in

Romans 13:14, 'put ... on the Lord Jesus Christ'.

As he spoke, Spurgeon seemed to be completely absorbed in his subject. The American had heard other preachers who seemed to point more to themselves than to Christ. The pastor of the Metropolitan Tabernacle was different, displaying transparent humility and 'self-forgetfulness'. He not only preached *about* Christlikeness, he seemed to actually *embody* that quality, even as he spoke. Also noteworthy was the fact that Spurgeon did not talk down to his hearers. 'He was, in all things, one with his people, and he made them understand and feel it.' When the service closed and the vast crowd slowly emptied out of the building, the visitor was convinced they went away carrying Spurgeon's sermon 'in their hearts'. If so, then there would have been thousands that morning that had caught a fresh vision of Christ, and of the difference he could make to their lives.

This description of an ordinary Tabernacle service gives us a window on to Spurgeon's regular Sunday ministry. It shows us that the services continued to be packed into the 1880s. Certainly this was the case in the 1860s and the 1870s, too. Also our report by a transatlantic visitor introduces the main theme of this chapter – that of wider ministry and writing. Clearly, Spurgeon wasn't only reaching Londoners, or even just people from Britain. He could rightly claim to have a global ministry. Of course, only a privileged few were able to come from overseas to hear Spurgeon in person. But

through the medium of print, his words were reaching not only America, but also right around the world.

Spurgeon's books

Only a sampling of Spurgeon's vast written output can be noted here. We've already mentioned some of his most important books: *Morning by Morning, Evening by Evening* and the multi-volume *Treasury of David*. Each of these had a rich, warm, devotional tone. *Morning by Morning* and its follow-up, *Evening by Evening*, were especially popular. Well-thumbed copies could be found in countless Victorian homes, where they were regularly used as aids to family prayers and personal Quiet Times. The two slim volumes soon came to be printed together, with the title *Morning and Evening*. In this form they are still used around the world today.

Spurgeon wrote a number of works which were especially geared to help fellow pastors and preachers. One example of this type of book was *Commenting and Commentaries*, first published in 1876. In this Spurgeon reviewed a vast range of biblical commentaries – nearly 4,000 in total. The survey was not only comprehensive, it was also lively. If he didn't like a commentary he wasn't afraid to say so! 'Says nothing of any consequence', 'Do not lumber your shelves with it', 'Useless', 'Rubbish' and 'Utter rubbish': these are just some of the ways in which Spurgeon dismissed various volumes. He was especially severe about anything that questioned the inspiration of Scripture. Works that were dry, dusty and dull also provoked his displeasure. But many commentaries were enthusiastically commended. He especially appreciated older Puritan commentaries, like those he had first encountered in the darkened room of his grandfather James's manse in Stambourne all those years ago. What attracted him to these works above all others was their obvious love for Scripture and their blend of deep theology, warm devotion and practical application. Spurgeon detected the

LEFT
A selection of publications written by Spurgeon
ABOVE
Spurgeon's book *The Way of Salvation*

note of authentic Christian experience sounding clearly down the centuries through these sixteenth- and seventeenth-century commentaries. He loved them for it, bemoaning the fact that many of the works of his own day did not bear comparison with these spiritual classics. These books had stood the test of time, and one of the marks of Spurgeon's writing is that it has stood the test of time as well. Just as *Morning and Evening* continues to be read, so many of today's preachers still refer to *Commenting and Commentaries*.

Spurgeon wrote a range of other books that are now less well known. At the other end of the scale from *Commenting and Commentaries* are two small books which, at the time, were among his most popular. The first of these was entitled *John Ploughman's Talk*. Spurgeon wrote as the imaginary John Ploughman, a farm labourer who dispensed 'plain advice for plain people' on a wide range of homely topics, not all of them specifically Christian. This proved so successful that another volume, *John Ploughman's Pictures*, soon followed. The opening words of *John Ploughman's Talk* – 'It is of no more use to give advice to the idle than to pour water into a sieve' – gives a flavour of the style Spurgeon adopted. All the early editions were illustrated with careful line drawings which enhanced the book's appeal. Spurgeon produced many other popular works, with titles such as *The Bible and the Newspaper, The Spare Half Hour* and *The Good Start* (which was especially for young people). No other Christian writer in the Victorian era was so popular with those society considered ordinary and unlearned.

But Spurgeon was read by all classes, and not just in the English-speaking world. In the Heritage Room at Spurgeon's College there is a small display case containing some of the foreign language editions of his works. These include translations into languages as varied as Arabic, Italian, Bengali and Welsh. Some of these only appeared after his death. But the work of translation and publication was already underway in his lifetime. Through his writing, Spurgeon did indeed have a wider ministry, and he would continue to speak from beyond the grave.

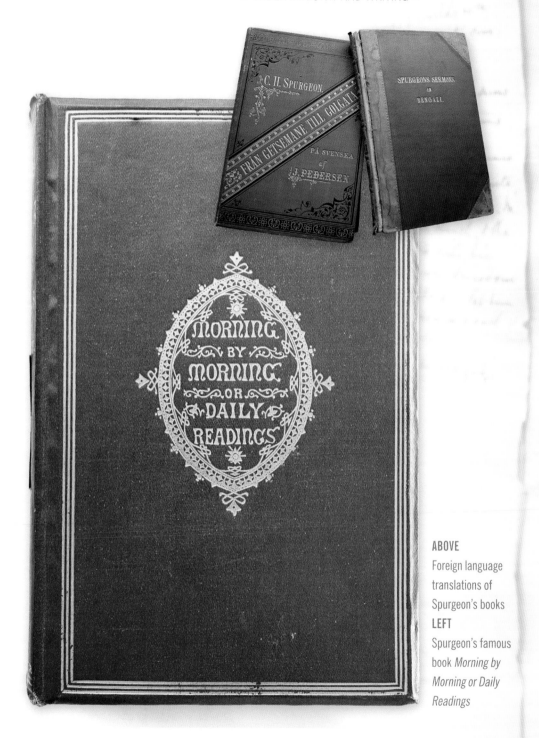

ABOVE
Foreign language translations of Spurgeon's books

LEFT
Spurgeon's famous book *Morning by Morning or Daily Readings*

The *Metropolitan Tabernacle Pulpit*

Important as Spurgeon's many and varied books were, it was through the medium of his printed sermons that he was best known, and best loved. We have already seen how, in 1855 when he was still only twenty-one, one of Spurgeon's messages began to be printed on a regular, weekly basis. The production of these was a major operation, involving many people in addition to the preacher. What was the process by which these sermons, preached on a Sunday from a few simple notes, reached the printed page?

Each week someone sat in the Tabernacle congregation and took down Spurgeon's message, word for word, in longhand. The many people who have enjoyed reading Spurgeon's sermons down the years owe them a significant debt. The preacher would be given these longhand notes on the Monday. These he would proceed to edit, usually quite lightly. The edited notes would then be typeset by his publishers. These were Passmore and Alabaster, who produced all of Spurgeon's books. Joseph Passmore was a deacon at the Tabernacle and Spurgeon trusted him implicitly. The next phase involved returning the draft printed pages to Spurgeon. Spurgeon would work from these galley proofs, doing any further editing he thought was required. It was the corrected galley proof that was the basis of the final published message. The *Metropolitan Tabernacle Pulpit* appeared every Thursday, price one penny. The process by which the preached sermon became the printed text was so well honed that Sunday's sermon could be available to buy and read before the week was out. Usually eight pages long, these small 'penny pulpits' were eagerly awaited the length and breadth of the land – and over the whole world.

Because Spurgeon usually preached three times a week at the Tabernacle – twice on Sunday and once during the week – there was

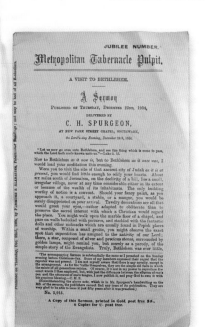

a large stock of sermons still unpublished at the time of his death. Production of the messages was carried on, and they continued to be as popular as ever. By the end of the nineteenth century, over one hundred million copies had been sold, translated into at least twenty-three different languages. The last printed sermon – number 3,563 – appeared on 10 May 1917. In 1905 it was estimated that if all the pages of Spurgeon's published sermons were placed end to end they could almost reach to the moon. Presumably, by 1917, enough copies of the *Metropolitan Tabernacle Pulpit* had been printed to bridge the remaining gap and make a landing! By any standards these are staggering statistics.

Spurgeon's influence

There are numerous accounts of how people were influenced by these messages. The stories come from the rich and famous and from the poor and anonymous; they come from every continent. Spurgeon was not only read privately, but also publicly, for often someone with a flair for reading would gather a 'congregation' and proceed to 'preach' Spurgeon's sermon to them. D.L. Moody said:

> It is a sight in Colorado on Sunday to see the miners come out of
> the bowels of the hills and gather in schoolhouses or under the trees
> while some old English miner stands up and reads one of Charles
> Spurgeon's sermons.

All around the world there were similar meetings, in houses and halls, on ships and in the open air. Spurgeon never visited America, Africa or Australasia. But in these great continents barely a day passed without someone, somewhere, preaching a Spurgeon sermon.

LEFT
A published sermon

ABOVE
Young Spurgeon with his publisher, Joseph Passmore

There were many conversions. As early as 1861, news reached the Tabernacle that eleven people had come to Christ in a town in New Zealand as a result of Spurgeon's messages. Some of those converted went on to become preachers and pastors themselves. A man from Tennessee wrote to Spurgeon that he, who had formerly been a 'wild young man', had become a Christian 'through reading one of Mr Spurgeon's sermons'. The man testified that he was now the pastor of a 'large and influential' church.

In addition to the conversions, there were many believers who were being built up in the faith. A minister based in St Petersburg, Russia, wrote to Spurgeon saying: 'You are having a part in the great work of spreading Christ's kingdom ... You are well known among the [Russian Orthodox] priests, who seem to get hold of your translated sermons.'

Spurgeon rejoiced in these stories, as did the Tabernacle congregation. This London church, which had been contemplating closure before Spurgeon's arrival, was now a means by which the gospel was proclaimed around the world.

One final story shows that Spurgeon's sermons not only bore fruit around the world, they could also be of use closer to home! Spurgeon said,

> [At one time] I felt very weary, very sad, and very heavy at heart; and I began to doubt in my own mind whether I really enjoyed the things I preached to others. It seemed to be a dreadful thing for me to be only a waiter, and not a guest, at the gospel feast. I went to a certain country town, and on the Sabbath day entered a Methodist chapel. The man who conducted the service was an engineer; he read the Scriptures, and prayed, and preached. The tears flowed freely from my eyes; I was moved to the deepest emotion by every sentence of the sermon, and I felt all my difficulty removed, for the gospel, I saw, was very dear to me, and had a wonderful effect on my own heart. I went to the preacher, and said, 'I thank you very much for that sermon.' He asked me who I was, and when I told him, he looked as red as possible, and he said, 'Why, it was one of your sermons that I preached this

This London church ... was now a means by which the gospel was proclaimed around the world

morning!' 'Yes,' I said, 'I know it was; but that was the very message I wanted to hear, because I then saw that I did enjoy the very Word I myself preached.' It was happily so arranged in the good providence of God. Had it been his own sermon, it would not have answered the purpose nearly so well as when it turned out to be one of mine.

Few people, it seems, were left untouched by Spurgeon's preaching! His ministry had a global reach and touched the deep places of people's hearts.

Digging deeper

Still much more could be said about Spurgeon and the printed word. For example, from 1865 he began issuing a monthly magazine, *The Sword and Trowel*, which contained articles, book reviews and much more. Spurgeon edited the magazine himself and contributed a significant number of the articles. *The Sword and Trowel* was widely read. And still we could go on.

So, once more the 'marvellous power' of God was at work, this time through the written word. The effect of Spurgeon's ministry cannot be adequately explained without regard to the importance of prayer and the power of the Holy Spirit. Certainly this was the view of Spurgeon and of his Tabernacle congregation. Reports of what was happening around the world were regularly fed back to the various Tabernacle prayer meetings, as an encouragement and as a further stimulus to prayer.

Engage

We live in an age where the 'visual' is all important. Every day we are bombarded by thousands upon thousands of images: through our TV screens, in magazines – wherever we look. In this context, it's vital we use the visual to communicate the Christian faith. But I often feel we underestimate the power of the written word (I know as a writer I'm biased!). Spurgeon's ministry shows us how effective words can be and he too lived in a time when the visual was significant. Many people from all classes regularly went to the theatre and the music hall, for example. Christian literature, including good quality fiction like C.S. Lewis's *Chronicles of Narnia* can build us up and be useful in commending Christ to others.

But, whatever means we use, do we work for the conversion of men and women and the building up of believers? And do we pray for this? This chapter encourages us to redouble our efforts in prayer, especially for all those involved in evangelism.

Further reflection on Spurgeon's example also challenges us about Christlikeness. John the Baptist, speaking about the Lord Jesus, said: 'He must increase, but I must decrease' (John 3:30, AV). The quality of self-forgetfulness which the American visitor to the Tabernacle noticed can be explained by Spurgeon's overriding desire to focus on Christ. He did not want people to leave his services saying 'What a great preacher!' – rather, he wanted them to look to Christ and say, 'What a great Saviour!'

Are we full of ourselves, or do we point people to Christ, as John the Baptist and Spurgeon did? We are called not just to pray for the conversion of others, important as that is. We are also called to point men and women, boys and girls, not to ourselves but to the Lord Jesus.

NOTES

1   The newspaper was *The Christian Advocate*, a New York-based Methodist paper. The report appeared on 13 October 1881.

2   This hymn was written by Elizabeth Scott in 1763. The chapel book was *Our Own Hymn Book* (London: Passmore and Alabaster, 1866), which Spurgeon edited himself.

CHAPTER 9

The Pastors' College

S WE continue to think about the theme of wider ministry, we turn to consider the work of the Pastors' College, now known as Spurgeon's College. Of all his various enterprises it was this, Spurgeon said, that was his 'first born and best beloved'. On one occasion he declared: 'This is my life's work, to which I believe … God has called me.'

The origins of the college go back to 1855 and Spurgeon's New Park Street days. It started with just one student, and there was little idea of how things might develop. But, by 1865, there were over 150 men actively engaged in mission and ministry who had received their training at the college.[1] From very small beginnings something had started which, like Spurgeon's writing and preaching ministry, was to have a major impact on the Christian world.

T.W. Medhurst and the beginnings of the Pastors' College

The first student was Thomas William Medhurst, who was from Bermondsey in south London. In many ways he was typical of the sort of students who would later come to the college in such numbers. Medhurst was young, practically the same age as Spurgeon himself. He was relatively poor, at the time of his conversion working as an apprentice rope maker. And he had received little formal education. His standard of spoken English left something to be desired – at least that was the view of some of the New Park Street members. For many in the Victorian age, Medhurst would have seemed very unpromising ministry material. Spurgeon, however, thought differently. His college would take many such men and equip them to serve churches and reach countless communities with the gospel.

Medhurst had, in fact, been converted through Spurgeon. The young rope maker had written to the pastor of New Park Street, anxiously asking: 'How am I to find Jesus? How am I to know that

ABOVE
The Pastors'
College Conference
1888 (Bottom
row, Seated,
second from left:
Charles Spurgeon;
Far right:
Thomas Medhurst)

He died for me?' Spurgeon took time out from his busy schedule to respond with great care and at length. At the close of his letter he said: 'There is the cross, and a bleeding God-man upon it; look to Him and be saved! There is the Holy Spirit able to give you every grace. Look, in prayer, to ... God, and then you will be delivered.' Spurgeon was speaking in terms that harked back to his own conversion. Medhurst did 'look to Christ' and receive salvation, to Spurgeon's great delight. The two men met, and Spurgeon had the joy of baptising the new convert, who joined New Park Street. The year was 1854.

Immediately Medhurst began preaching in the grim, polluted streets surrounding the chapel. He was full of zeal, but some New Park Street members who heard him were shocked at what they called his 'want of education'. They felt strongly enough to complain to Spurgeon. Medhurst should be stopped! But Medhurst's response when Spurgeon met him was to say: 'I must preach, sir; and I shall preach unless you cut off my head!' Spurgeon was suitably impressed. This was the sort of talk he liked. When he reported back to the New Park Street deacons they all agreed that Medhurst's head should stay firmly attached to his shoulders! Soon two people were converted through the young man's street preaching and joined New Park Street themselves. Spurgeon took notice and told Medhurst he believed God was calling him to be a preacher and a pastor. The logical next step would be for Medhurst to go to college.

Of course, we remember that Spurgeon did not undergo any formal training before *he* became a minister. But Spurgeon himself recognised that he was a fairly unique character, and that others would benefit from some theological education. Certainly he believed this was important for Medhurst. But what was the best way forward for his friend? If truth be told, Spurgeon was unimpressed by what was on offer from the different colleges which sought to train pastors. He felt they downplayed the robust biblical theology to which he was so strongly attached. Also, they were not focused enough on the practical issues of mission and ministry. For Medhurst, there would be additional problems. Colleges were expensive, and they assumed that incoming students would already have a fairly good standard of education. On both counts the young street preacher would be struggling. Spurgeon decided on what for him was the obvious solution. He would train Medhurst himself.

So, in July 1855, Thomas Medhurst began to study under his pastor's supervision, with Spurgeon paying for the student's board and lodging out of his own pocket. This went well, but if the work was to expand, as Spurgeon now hoped it would, it was not a workable solution long term. With financial help from two of his deacons, including William Olney, Spurgeon was now ready to take on a second student. The year was 1856, and what would be known as the Pastors' College was now well and truly underway.[2]

The college grows

Spurgeon needed someone to act as a tutor. The man he chose, George Rogers, was a Congregational minister. Rogers' appointment to this crucial post might seem a little surprising as, like Spurgeon's father and grandfather, he practised infant baptism. But in other respects he and Spurgeon were of one mind. Rogers was committed to biblical doctrine, loved the Puritans, was a good teacher and had the ability to relate well to young people. Spurgeon also recognised in Rogers a man who was earnest and deeply devout. These last qualities were absolutely essential because Spurgeon was determined that the spiritual zeal of the incoming students should increase, not decrease. He was suspicious that some colleges took rough and ready evangelists and turned them into what he called 'sapless' essay writers! What was the use of someone who could excel in academic assignments but who had lost their love for God and passion for souls? No! In his college the training would be practical and the 'first place' would be given to 'spiritual fervour'. The zeal of a man like Medhurst might need to be channelled, but it must not be quenched. In Rogers, Spurgeon thought he had found just the man to help him carry this vision forward.

The college's base of operations now switched to Rogers' home. This was spacious enough to accommodate the growing numbers of students, at least for a few years. The college was almost unique in that it did not require applicants to sit an entrance examination to show that they were fit to study. If this had been the case, some of those who went on to be successful pastors would

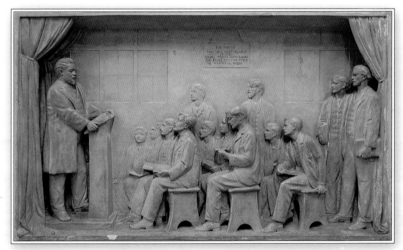

RIGHT
Stone carving of Spurgeon speaking to his students
FAR RIGHT
The room where Spurgeon gave his famous Friday afternoon lectures at the Pastors' College

probably have fallen at the first hurdle. Instead, Spurgeon and Rogers looked for a cluster of qualities. Prospective students had to be humble and willing to learn. They had to show some evidence of gifting in preaching, evangelism and pastoral work, together with a clear call from God to pursue this further. Spurgeon was adamant that *he* couldn't make pastors and evangelists – only *God* could do that. He would take those whom the Lord was calling and help them realise their potential. Spurgeon and Rogers also wanted to see that a potential student had a love for people, both Christian and non-Christian. Finally, there had to be evidence of a deep spirituality – a real love for the Lord. Many, including those who had been commended by their home churches, failed these exacting tests and were turned away. There may have been no entrance exam, but that did not mean that getting into the college was easy.

Rogers proved to be all that Spurgeon had hoped and more. He was extremely effective, first as tutor and then, as the college expanded and more staff were added, as principal. He was not only respected; he was loved by successive generations of students. Spurgeon continued as president of the college and remained actively involved week by week.

After the first few years, meeting in Rogers' home became increasingly unworkable: everything was just too cramped. Fortunately, from 1861, the college was able to use basement rooms in the newly opened Metropolitan Tabernacle. Financially, things were often difficult. The college was undoubtedly a venture of faith. But as Spurgeon and his friends trusted and prayed, the work continued to grow.

Teaching at the college

What curriculum did the students study? To begin with, an important place was given to basic education. Those who struggled with subjects such as Mathematics and English were given the extra help they required. Depending on the needs of individuals, considerable time might be given to this foundational work. Those who didn't need it could progress at a faster pace. But, of course, the key subjects for all students were the Bible and Christian doctrine, which were covered in depth. All those exiting the college should have a thorough knowledge of the Scriptures and of the great themes of the Christian Church. There was also some Church history, together with detailed instruction in preaching and the general 'conduct of church work'. The tone of every session was geared to fostering the zeal and commitment of the students. The training, taken as a whole, had a single, overarching aim: to equip the men for a lifetime's gospel ministry. Students were to be given the biblical, theological and practical tools so they could do the work God had called them to.

These priorities were embodied in the lectures Spurgeon himself gave to the students. Every Friday afternoon he would speak on a different aspect of Christian ministry. These talks were always eagerly anticipated. When Spurgeon, who was known by students as the 'Guv'nor', arrived, he was usually greeted by enthusiastic clapping and cheering! The college president enjoyed these times as much as the students. He was as relaxed with them, he reckoned, as he was with his own family. Perhaps because of this, there was plenty of laughter in these sessions.

On one occasion, Spurgeon imitated the mannerisms of some of the different preachers he had seen and heard. These included someone continually whirling their arms like a mechanical windmill, and another thumping the pulpit for the entire length of his sermon, like a 'never-ceasing hammer'. Such 'jerking, sawing, pumping and pounding' detracted from the message and, said Spurgeon sternly, was to be avoided at all costs. To the delight of the students, he said:

> It has occurred to me that some speakers fancy they are beating carpets, or chopping sticks, or mincing sausage-meat, or patting

... he was usually greeted by enthusiastic clapping and cheering!

butter, or poking their fingers into people's eyes. Oh, could they see themselves as others see them, they might cease thus to perform before the public, and save their bodily exercise for other occasions!

When these Friday afternoon talks were published under the title *Lectures to my Students*, Spurgeon commissioned an artist to draw pictures of these preachers in action, and these were included in the book. Many congregations, as well as many preachers, were thankful that Spurgeon had addressed these issues.

On other Fridays, Spurgeon could open his very heart to the students. He once spoke about how ministers were, in his view, especially prone to depression. Of course, he was speaking from personal experience. He shared how, in the aftermath of the Surrey Gardens music hall disaster, his life had been a waking nightmare, a seemingly never-ending horror. Only the realisation that Jesus was still with him had got him through. Movingly, he told his students that if any of them were to experience a similar catastrophe they too could continue to trust in their faithful Lord Jesus. He was able to pilot them through any storm, no matter how strong it might become. Years later, former students would remember the Friday lectures with the Guv'nor as the highlight of their college experience.

Life at the college

Most theological colleges at this time were residential – students lived on campus. But the Pastors' College had no campus and, anyway, Spurgeon's vision was different. The trainee ministers all stayed with different families from the Tabernacle, an arrangement that Spurgeon believed helped keep them in touch with everyday life. The college president was always keen to keep the closest possible connections between classroom, church and wider world. Students were expected to attend Tabernacle prayer meetings and participate in church life in other ways. They also preached regularly in chapels and mission halls, in London and further afield. In fact, they were in great demand as speakers – but this created a problem. Some churches sought to call these students to be their ministers *before* their course was completed. Spurgeon complained that his charges were being enticed away from the college before they were ready. But clearly there was something about the training that was being given which met the real needs of the day. Ministers were being shaped who were well suited to the work of practical ministry.

The numbers being accepted for training steadily increased – fourteen in 1865; twenty-five in 1866; thirty-seven in 1867. Now it was the basement rooms at the Tabernacle which were becoming cramped. They had never been entirely suitable in the first place. They were dark, dingy and depressing. Because of the lack of natural light, the gas lamps had to be kept burning all day. As we have seen, the air quality above ground in London was not great. Here in the Tabernacle basement it could be almost intolerable. The fumes from the lights and the lack of ventilation made it difficult to concentrate and even affected the health of some students. To the relief of everyone (not least Spurgeon, who hated these conditions), in 1874 the college was able to move to new purpose-built premises in nearby Temple Street. This was where the work stayed until, in 1923, Spurgeon's College moved to its present site on South Norwood Hill. This is near where the old Crystal Palace stood, and is also close to the site of 'Westwood', the house in which Charles and Susannah lived from 1880. So the area is steeped in 'Spurgeonic' history! The college seeks to draw from this rich history as it trains evangelical gospel ministers for a new day and generation.

The influence of the college

By the time the Temple Street buildings had been opened, a constant stream of committed evangelical gospel ministers were being sent out each year. Some of these went to established churches and some went to pioneer new works in difficult neighbourhoods around Britain, often with startling success. Still others went overseas. In fact, by 1878, Spurgeon was able to report that former students had gone out to the 'four corners of the globe'. Italy, India, Japan, Australia ... These were just a few of the places where pastors, church planters and evangelists were working. Like their counterparts in Britain, these cross-cultural missionaries, shaped by the distinctive values of the college, were often the means of significant church growth.

One student who demonstrated the global reach of the college was Thomas Johnson, who began study in 1875. Johnson was an American and one of the first black men to study at Spurgeon's. His story is a remarkable one. He was a former slave and had already been a pastor in Denver, Colorado. But he felt called to go as a missionary to Africa, and wanted further training. Deeply impressed with Spurgeon's sermons, which he would regularly quote from the pulpit, Thomas Johnson came to London, together with his wife, Henrietta. Thomas was forty years of age and nervous about study. But the other students, and especially Spurgeon himself (who was vehemently opposed to enslavement in all its forms), helped him feel he was among friends. Johnson wrote of his first meeting with Spurgeon:

> His first words set me at ease, but his sympathetic kindness was beyond my highest hope. He took me by the hand, asked me a few questions and wished me success ... I felt I had been talking to a dear loving friend. I at once fell in love with dear Mr Spurgeon ... I felt so happy in his presence, and so at home with him, that I could not help saying, 'Well, thank God he is my friend.'

Regarding his overall college experience, he said: 'I can truthfully and gladly say that I had never been treated more kindly or made to feel more at home and happy than when at the Pastors' College'. Thomas Johnson's motto was 'Africa for Jesus', and his desire to minister there was realised. He and another Afro-American student, Calvin Richardson, together with their wives, sailed for West Africa in 1878. They travelled through Sierra Leone and Liberia before settling

... students had gone out to the 'four corners of the globe'

in Cameroon. Tragically, Henrietta Johnson died of a fever in March 1879, having previously nursed her husband through a similar attack. Thomas himself became unwell again, and there was little option but to leave Africa. But the Richardsons remained and in 1886 were still working in Cameroon.

Not all of Spurgeon's students were as pioneering as these two brave and committed couples. But the vast majority who had undergone training became engaged in fruitful gospel work. If Johnson's inspiring dictum had been 'Africa for Jesus', the college had a motto of its own. In Latin this was *Et Teneo Et Teneor*, which translates as 'I hold and am held'. Those who held on to the cross of Christ found that God was also holding on to them. So the students were sustained for a lifetime's fruitful ministry.

And what became of Thomas Medhurst, Spurgeon's first-ever student? Spurgeon always felt a deep affection for the young man who, by saying he'd rather die than stop preaching, had started it all. Medhurst held pastorates in Kingston in west London, Coleraine in Ireland, Glasgow in Scotland, and Lake Road in Portsmouth: not exactly the four corners of the globe, but almost the four corners of the British Isles![3] During his ministry, he baptised almost 1,000 people. Spurgeon once went to take a service at a place where Medhurst was well known, but where he himself had rarely preached. To his amusement, at the close of the service he overheard the following conversation:

'Well, how did you like Mr Spurgeon?'
'Oh, very well; but I would have enjoyed the service more if he hadn't imitated our dear Mr Medhurst so much!'

Medhurst's preaching style clearly owed rather a lot to Spurgeon, even if the former student's regular hearers didn't realise it!

🛈 Digging deeper

If we wanted to summarise the sort of training the Pastors' College sought to provide we could perhaps say it had three closely interwoven strands. First of all, Spurgeon wanted students to grow in *knowledge*. For sure, this was not merely head knowledge. Spurgeon would have been the first to say that truth had to fire the heart as well as inform the mind. But he did want students to grow in understanding – of the Bible, Christian doctrine, Christian history and much else besides. What's more, Spurgeon hoped to encourage those he trained to develop a taste for lifelong learning. He could read up to six 'difficult' books a week and had a personal library of over 10,000 volumes. It was unlikely that any student would reach his standard or, for that matter, have space to house so many books. But Spurgeon wanted them to continue to study after they had left college. This was important if they were going to enjoy long and effective Christian ministries.

If the first strand was the importance of knowledge, the second was the development of *gifts*. Spurgeon was quite clear that ministry gifts came from God, and God alone. Nevertheless, they were like muscles that needed to grow strong through use, or like tools that needed to be sharpened. The Pastors' College helped students to develop in using their gifts: good preachers became better, useful evangelists became even more effective, good pastors learnt how to care for people in even more helpful ways. Through the teaching and through the opportunities to put what they were learning into practice, the students sharpened their gifts, and perhaps discovered that God was giving them new ones, too.

The final strand was that of *godliness*. Spurgeon knew that gifts without godliness would lead to disaster. Charisma and character had to go together. It almost goes without saying that this, for Spurgeon, was absolutely crucial. Finally, binding the three strands together was an absolute reliance on the work of the Holy Spirit. In 1875 Spurgeon wrote the following to the students:

> Without the Spirit, you will be failures, and worse; therefore pray much, and see to it that your whole selves are in such a condition that the Spirit of God can dwell in you; for in some … He cannot work. Let the channel through which the living water is to flow be clear and clean … I feel in agony when I imagine any one of you going forth to preach unendowed by the Spirit. The Lord alone knows how I have the work of the college on my heart … If souls are not won, and churches not built up, and Christ is not glorified by you, I have lived in vain as to the master-work of my life.

But Spurgeon's work had *not* been in vain. It certainly bore fruit in the nineteenth century. The priorities he established for training, where they are faithfully practised, will continue to bear fruit today.

🔢 Engage

Not all are called to be pastors, cross-cultural missionaries, paid evangelists or so-called 'full-time' church workers. Spurgeon recognised this, and affirmed it strongly. What was important was that people lived for Christ wherever He had placed them. Labourers, homemakers, shopkeepers, builders, shoemakers: all these occupations and more were vital avenues for Christian service. What was crucial, according to Spurgeon, was that people lived for God whatever their calling and situation in life. In a very real sense all of us are to be 'full-time' for the Lord, and Spurgeon's vision for training – growth in knowledge, in gifts and in godliness – is one which applies to us all.

How is God calling you to grow in knowledge and understanding? What gifts has He given you that you're not really using? Finally, are you growing in godliness? It's easy for us to stagnate spiritually, especially if we've been Christians for some time. But God doesn't want us to do this. Whatever our calling, whatever our age, whatever our situation in life – one thing is sure: God calls us to *grow*.

NOTES

1 Women were not trained until the latter decades of the twentieth century. Now, the college is fully committed to train both women and men for Christian ministry and mission. For those who want to find out more about the history of the college, there is an excellent recent book by Ian Randall, *A School of the Prophets: 150 Years of Spurgeon's College* (London: Spurgeon's College, 2005).

2 The name became official in 1868.

3 Which then included the whole of Ireland.

LEFT
Spurgeon's College today, based in South Norwood
OVER THE PAGE
Stained-glass window showing the college motto

ET
TENEO ET
TENEOR

CHAPTER 10

The Stockwell Orphanage

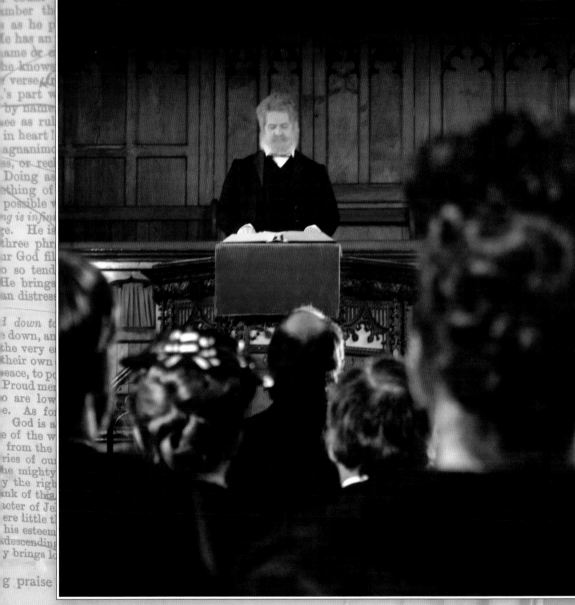

'HE greatest sermon Mr. Spurgeon ever preached' was how William Young Fullerton described the orphanage that Spurgeon built at Stockwell, south London.[1] Given what we've seen concerning the impact of his Sunday ministry this is some statement! How can it be true that an *orphanage* was Spurgeon's greatest sermon when his actual messages transformed the lives of people on every continent? But Spurgeon's orphanage also transformed the lives of many people. These were boys and girls whose lives would otherwise have been utterly miserable and, in all probability, very short. Of course, it wasn't a sermon in the conventional sense, but it did speak volumes of God's love in action.

The story of the Stockwell Orphanage was, just like the Pastors' College, a wonderful adventure of faith, a story in which prayer and perseverance were present in equal measure. And, just like the messages in the *Metropolitan Tabernacle Pulpit*, the orphanage came to be spoken of throughout the world.

Beginnings

It will probably come as no surprise that the orphanage really began in a prayer meeting. In August 1866, during one of the regular Monday night prayer times at the Tabernacle, Spurgeon had declared:

> 'Dear friends, we are a huge church, and should be doing more for the Lord in this great city. I want us, tonight, to ask Him to send us *some new work* and if we need money to carry it on, let us pray that *the means also be sent*.'

Given the many different ministries Spurgeon and the church were already engaged in, this was a pretty amazing statement! But Spurgeon was never one to rest on his laurels, and was always looking for new ways to serve his Lord. A number of those present then led the meeting in prayer, asking God for guidance. One of these was deacon William Olney. It appears that it was while Olney was wrestling in prayer that Spurgeon felt sure God was going to answer, and that they could now leave things with Him. Spurgeon directed that they should turn to pray for other subjects. As far as the 'new work' was concerned, all that was necessary now was to wait for God's answer to come.

Just a few days later, Spurgeon received an unusual letter from a Mrs Anne Hillyard, a clergyman's widow. Anne Hillyard knew of Spurgeon through *The Sword and Trowel* and by personal recommendation. In her letter she was offering to give a substantial amount of money for a specific purpose: the 'training and education of a few orphan boys'. Spurgeon was astonished at the sum she appeared willing to donate. He and William Higgs, one of his deacons and a builder by trade, met Mrs Hillyard to discuss her proposal. The two men decided to be careful and began by saying they wanted to talk about the £200 Anne had written about in her letter.

The widow was shocked. 'Did I write £200? I meant £20,000.'

'Oh yes,' Spurgeon replied, 'you did put down £20,000, but I was not sure whether a nought or two had slipped in by mistake, and thought I would be on the safe side!'

At a rough calculation, Anne Hillyard was offering the equivalent of about £1,300,000 in today's money.[2] Was this the answer to prayer for which Spurgeon had been waiting?

As the meeting proceeded, Spurgeon remained cautious. Was there no living relative who ought to receive at least some of this? No? Then why not give it to George Muller in Bristol, for *his* home for orphans? This was a work which was already well established and which was, in Spurgeon's view, an extremely worthy cause. The mention at this point of Muller, whose story can be read in *Robber of the Cruel Streets*[3], is interesting. Historians don't often put Spurgeon and Muller together, but in fact the two were good friends. Spurgeon greatly admired Muller, describing him as a man 'mighty in prayer', who had repeatedly 'tried and proved the promises of God'. Spurgeon was certain that Muller would put the money to good use! But Anne Hillyard was insistent. Spurgeon himself must establish a home. At last the pastor of the Metropolitan Tabernacle was satisfied. He would receive the money and an orphanage would be built. This was only the beginning, but Spurgeon was convinced that God was in this project. The prayers of the Monday night meeting had been answered.

Countless people would contribute financially to the establishment and ongoing development of Spurgeon's orphanage. But, humanly speaking, without Anne Hillyard the project would never have got off the ground. Throughout her lifetime she shunned the limelight, preferring to remain as anonymous as possible. She moved to Bath and, when she died in January 1880, it was only with difficulty that the orphanage Trustees were able to discover her address. The work always remained close to her heart and her last words were reputed to have been, 'My boys! My boys!' Her gift was commemorated in a stained-glass window in the orphanage boardroom. This depicted her first and fateful meeting with Spurgeon and Higgs and also carried the text of James 1:27 which, in the Authorised Version, speaks of looking after the 'fatherless ... in their affliction'. The verse was obviously appropriate. Anne Hillyard was not an 'up front' person, but she willingly offered to God what she could and a wonderful ministry was the result. Her sacrificial giving stands as an example – and a challenge – to us.

Was this the answer to prayer for which Spurgeon had been waiting?

The boys' and girls' houses

Once Spurgeon accepted a task he threw himself into it lock, stock and barrel. Things now moved quickly. Before 1867 was out a board of Trustees had been formed, with Spurgeon himself in the chair. Charles's brother, James Archer Spurgeon, was a Trustee. So effective was James's work that in January 1868, he was invited to be assistant pastor at the Tabernacle to further ease the burden on his brother. He was by no means as effective a preacher as Charles, but he was an able administrator and gave invaluable help.

With the Spurgeon brothers now working together on the orphanage, and many able deacons at the Tabernacle also involved, plans were forging ahead. Land was purchased and foundation stones for new buildings laid. Charles Spurgeon wasted no time in setting the needs of the proposed orphanage before his ever-expanding support base, making particular use of *The Sword and Trowel*. People gave generously in response to the appeals. The *Autobiography* records a number of generous gifts, ranging from £250 to £1,000. One of these was from a Mrs Tyson, who would later leave £25,000 to the orphanage in her will. Many smaller gifts were no less sacrificial. All was needed, for financially things were tight. Much of Anne Hillyard's money was tied up in investments to which the Trustees did not have immediate access and this made things difficult. But they managed – just. The site which had been chosen was in Stockwell, about two miles to the west of the Elephant and Castle and the main Tabernacle buildings. Through 1868 and 1869 the builders were working and an impressive complex began to take shape. Finally, on 9 September 1869, amidst scenes of great celebration, the Stockwell Orphanage was officially opened.

Anne Hillyard's initial vision had been for 'fatherless boys', but Charles Spurgeon had always looked forward to the day when girls would be able to join them. Anne had been the first to make a donation towards this, giving £50 (presumably her financial resources were now largely exhausted!). This was an amount which Spurgeon himself immediately matched. Once again, generous support from readers of *The Sword and Trowel*, and from the Tabernacle congregation, made up the shortfall. It was in 1879 that a separate wing for girls was finally opened.

Throughout Spurgeon's lifetime the work continued to grow – when the girls' wing was completed there was space for 500 children. How could all this be financed? Spurgeon was inspired by the way Muller relied on faith and prayer. Spurgeon was more willing than Muller to make needs known but, in other respects, their approaches were very similar – as were their stories of answered prayer.

RIGHT
Spurgeon's
orphanage
from the
Illustrated News

Faith and prayer

One such answer to prayer came with the selection of the first headmaster. A man had been appointed who seemed to be eminently suitable. But he wrote to withdraw not long before he was due to take up his post. Spurgeon read the letter with dismay. What were they going to do? He did not have to wait long for the answer. Vernon Charlesworth – like George Rogers, the tutor at the Pastors' College, a Congregational minister – was visiting Spurgeon later the same week. Seeing Spurgeon's disappointment, Charlesworth confessed his own interest in the work and his willingness to take it on himself. Spurgeon knew Charlesworth well and took this to be the 'overruling hand of God'. Vernon Charlesworth was quickly appointed!

Neither Spurgeon nor the orphanage children had cause to regret the decision. Charlesworth was a godly man who was conscientious regarding all aspects of his work. Moreover, he was loved by successive generations of children. Other staff came and went but the headmaster remained at his post until his death in

1914 – a remarkable forty-four years of service. Spurgeon did not know this when he wrote, in 1869, that 'he was filled with gratitude' to God for Charlesworth's appointment.

Other answers to prayer came by way of financial provision. 'If we get to the bottom of the barrel of meal,' Spurgeon once declared, 'the Lord will hear the scraping and then he will fill it up again!' As far as the orphanage finances were concerned, this was their experience year after year. On one occasion, Spurgeon remarked to the Trustees: 'Well, we're cleared out; we must go to the great Chancellor of the Exchequer!' Everyone present knew what he meant and immediately they turned to prayer. Within a few days £850 had been given to meet the most pressing needs. At another time someone presented Charlesworth with six dozen bunches of turnips, and expressed the hope that someone would send some mutton so the headmaster and children would have some meat to go with the vegetables. About an hour later, a farmer who had no idea of the previous gift sent the orphanage a whole sheep! Not surprisingly, such instances proved a great encouragement to continued prayer. This did not mean that life was easy and there were times when even Spurgeon's faith was sorely tested. But year by year they were not only able to manage, but also to develop the work. Spurgeon declared that the 'remarkable circumstances attending the founding and growth of this institution prove it to be the Lord's own work'. This is a judgment with which it is hard to disagree.

Spurgeon and his friends believed that God had called them to this work. Accordingly they had faith, were willing to take risks, and were diligent in prayer. Also, they were in this for the long haul, and persevered through disappointments and hardships. This is a real challenge for us; what is God calling us to give ourselves to, and how are we growing in faith, prayer, commitment and perseverance?

RIGHT
Stained-glass
window from the
orphanage

'Spurgeon's children'

Spurgeon was absolutely clear from the outset that places at Stockwell were to be allocated on the basis of need alone. Denominational allegiance was considered irrelevant and a significant number of children had Anglican backgrounds. His motto was simple: 'Always let the greatest need have the loudest voice.' Having said this, many children were not orphans in the strictest sense of the term as their mothers were still alive. Usually the father had died, leaving the widow and her children in a precarious situation. Of course, with no welfare state, if a father – the main breadwinner – did die, then even a middle-class family could quickly slide towards poverty if relatives were unable to step in and help. And such deaths were not uncommon in the polluted, disease-ridden, harsh streets of Victorian London. Spurgeon himself summed up the situation:

> The objects of our care are not far to seek. They are at our gates; widows worn down with labour, often pale, emaciated, delicate, and even consumptive;[4] children half-famished, growing up neglected, surrounded with temptation! Can you look at them without pity? We cannot!

Spurgeon looked at such families with deep compassion. And he didn't just look – he was also ready to act.

Some of the children concerned were from large families. A mother might be able to provide for some but not all of her offspring. Spurgeon's own upbringing had been very different from the Dickensian situation of many of those he was now in a position to help. But did he perhaps remember the time when his own mother and father had been unable to cope, and sent *him* to live with his grandparents? What is certain is that through his orphanage he was now in a position to transform the lives of thousands of boys and girls.

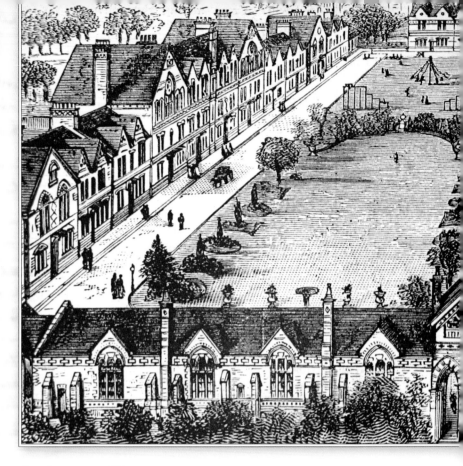

Orphanage life

What was life like for these children?[5] Spurgeon was determined
that the orphanage would be as little like an institution as possible.
First of all, the children did not wear a uniform. Children from
other orphanages were often distinguished from those living
with families because they wore easily recognisable uniforms –
they were known by the 'colour of their coats' as the saying went.
Spurgeon's children wore ordinary clothes and no two were dressed
alike. The Stockwell Orphanage was broken down into separate
'houses' arranged around a quadrangle. Most of these houses had
room for between twenty and thirty children, and each had a
housemistress and an assistant. This again was different to other
orphanages where children were accommodated in much larger
halls which sometimes resembled army barracks. Other work was
done to encourage a family atmosphere. There were regular days
out, alongside the ongoing programme of education. Sometimes

entertainers were brought in. For example, on Christmas day in 1877 the boys were treated to a Punch and Judy show and also a magic show. Much of this was both radical and enlightened. Christian love was shown not just by *taking in* needy children – it was also shown through the standard of care these children received once they had arrived.

Spurgeon was fully involved in the life of the orphanage. Not only did he remain as a very active chair of Trustees, he also visited the orphanage regularly. The news of his arrival was invariably greeted with a loud cheer! After Spurgeon's death, Charlesworth wrote:

> The children loved him; and his visits always called forth the most boisterous demonstrations of delight … The eagerness with which they sought to grasp his hand often involved the younger children in the risk of being trampled upon by the others.

Spurgeon himself remembered the boys and girls swarming around him 'like bees'. The priority he gave to this work is perhaps shown in that he would often find time to visit on Christmas day. And perhaps his popularity was enhanced by the fact that he would usually bring pennies to give to the children! But undoubtedly he was really loved – and not without reason. The children would have been aware of what their lives would have been like if it hadn't been for the orphanage. Their debt to him was much greater than a few pennies.

Anne Hillyard's vision had at its heart a commitment to give children every opportunity to respond to the Christian gospel. 'Bringing the little ones to Jesus is my first and chief desire', she had written. It comes as no surprise that this was a commitment Spurgeon wholeheartedly endorsed. On Sundays, children attended church services or, if they were considered too young, went to a specially arranged service at the orphanage. There was a Sunday school in the afternoon (as was the custom in Victorian times) and a Wednesday night meeting too. There was no pressure and certainly not all the children became Christians, although many of them did.

Two boys

Accounts from individual orphanage children from Spurgeon's lifetime are frustratingly few. I have not been able to find any from girls, but there are a few accounts from boys, and more information on two of them in particular.

John Maynard was known in the orphanage as 'little Jack'. He came to Christ whilst at Stockwell, and was baptised. He then entered the Pastors' College to train for ministry. On leaving the college he went to the Congo (now the Democratic Republic of Congo) to engage in cross-cultural mission. But Maynard had only been at Underhill Station on the Congo River for a few weeks when he fell ill with a fever. In 1886, the college and orphanage received the sad news of Maynard's death. He was just twenty-four years of age. A memorial tablet was erected in the dining hall for 'little Jack' who 'took the short route to heaven'. His story was told and retold to other orphanage children as an example of Christian commitment.

One child who heard the story of John Maynard was George Henry Edwards, who was at Stockwell between 1884 and 1890. A series of fourteen letters from George to his mother survive.[6] They provide a fascinating and moving insight into life at the orphanage. When George first arrived at Stockwell he was clearly unwell, perhaps malnourished, but he was soon able to write that his 'feet and hands' were better. His letters are full of little details – 'please bring me a penny box of crayons'; 'I had a letter from Aunt Ellen yesterday and she sent me a pair of gloves and a pair of mitts'; 'We go to Clapham Common sometimes in the afternoon and I like that very much'. In early letters, the spelling and grammar is sometimes wrong ('crayons' was actually spelt 'craons'), but this quickly improved. His handwriting is beautifully clear; in fact, it's far easier to read than Spurgeon's own! George understandably

LEFT
Spurgeon's memorial at the Stockwell Orphange

missed his natural family. But there is no reason to doubt that the words he wrote in the very first letter in the collection – 'I am very happy here' – remained true for the whole time of his stay.

In one letter, George recorded news of one of Spurgeon's own visits (on 11 March 1886). On this occasion, Spurgeon was treated to a gymnastic display from some of the boys. But more important (at least it would have been far more important to Spurgeon himself) was the information George had put in an earlier letter. In October 1885, George heard a Christian talk by a visiting speaker. A number of boys clearly made professions of faith on this occasion and George was among them. The names of those who had made commitments were taken down. George wrote that the speaker had promised 'to give us a book each' and had already passed on a 'little track' (he must have meant 'tract') called *The New Heart*. And it was on Wednesday 15 February 1888 that George listened to a talk about Africa, accompanied by magic lantern slides. One of the pictures he saw was of John Maynard. George wrote that some of the students from the college were there and it may have been them that took the session. George Edwards may not have followed Maynard's example of missionary service, but it appears both boys received 'new hearts' from God (see Ezekiel 36:26).

Spurgeon's orphanage had been the means by which vulnerable children had been rescued from disease and destitution. It had also been the means by which children had the opportunity to hear, and respond, to the gospel of Jesus Christ. Thus, many were rescued from spiritual poverty, and the original vision of Spurgeon and Anne Hillyard was wonderfully fulfilled.

🔍 Digging deeper

So, was the orphanage 'the greatest sermon Spurgeon ever preached' as Fullerton maintained? Someone might argue that this is nonsense, because Spurgeon's sermons are still read around the world today. They weren't just fruitful *then*, in the nineteenth century; they're also effective *now*, in the twenty-first. Of course

... was the orphanage 'the greatest sermon Spurgeon ever preached'...?

this is true, but the orphanage work which Spurgeon began continues to be effective today as well. The last orphanage closed its doors in 1979, but 'Spurgeons' (formerly Spurgeon's Childcare) continues to work with vulnerable children and young people. A whole range of creative projects are run across the UK in partnership with churches, local authorities and other bodies. Spurgeon not only established an orphanage, he laid the foundations for a work which would stand the test of time. Perhaps even Spurgeon would have agreed with Fullerton's statement, for he once visited Muller's Homes in Bristol and declared: 'I never heard such a sermon in my life as I saw there.'

But, of course, we don't need to decide between the *preaching* of Spurgeon, as contained in the *Metropolitan Tabernacle Pulpit*, and the bold statement of *love in action* which was the orphanage. Both were important and, in fact, they complemented one another. For Spurgeon there was no need to choose between the so-called social gospel and the offer of individual, personal salvation through faith in Jesus. He stood in an evangelical tradition which emphasised the need for both. It was vital that men and women, boys and girls, responded to make Jesus their personal Lord and Saviour. But it was also vital that Christian discipleship was worked out by showing social concern in the world. Spurgeon sought to have this dual emphasis in his own ministry, as he proclaimed the need for personal salvation *and* cared for widows and orphans. As churches and individual disciples, we are called to have the same emphases running through our lives today.

Engage

There have been times in the past when evangelicals have lost the emphasis on social action. Some have been anxious that if this *is* stressed, the importance of calling men and women to repentance and faith will fade into the background. But Spurgeon shows us this need not be the case. And not just Spurgeon, for other great heroes of the faith were also able to marry practical Christian love and evangelistic passion. As well as George Muller, these include George Whitefield, Hannah More and William Wilberforce to name but a few. Why not find out more about some of these people? All of them, in different ways, held together vigorous gospel preaching with active social concern. Rather than being a denial of the faith, practical social action is part of the birthright of all evangelical Christians.

Thankfully, in recent days many evangelicals *have* rediscovered the importance of love in action and have reasserted the need for this. You and your church may already be involved socially, both globally and locally. If so, I hope you've been encouraged to keep going! But maybe you're not involved in such work, or haven't even seen the need for it. In that case, I hope the material in this chapter has made you aware of the exciting possibilities of loving others for Jesus' sake. Who can you show the love of Christ to today? In your particular context, what could *you* do? Take some time to pray this through – but don't *just* pray. For if we're really following the example of Spurgeon, then our prayers will certainly lead on into action.

NOTES

1 W.Y. Fullerton, *C.H. Spurgeon: A Biography* (London: Williams and Norgate, 1920), p.246.

2 It appears she had inherited most of this money from one of her uncles. For anyone interested in finding out more about Anne Hillyard, née Field, there is an old article which contains some additional information. F.W. Thompson, 'The Morgans of Birmingham', *Baptist Quarterly*, Vol 2, No. 6, April 1925. See especially pp.263–267.

3 Clive Langmead, *Robber of the Cruel Streets: The Prayerful Life of George Muller* (Farnham: CWR, 2006). To accompany the book there is a DVD docudrama of the same name, a CTA Production.

4 That is, they had tuberculosis.

5 For further information on 'Spurgeon's children', see P. Shepherd, 'Spurgeon's Children', *Baptist Quarterly*, Vol 42, No. 2, April 2007, pp.89–102.

6 These are in the archives of 'Spurgeons', formerly Spurgeon's Childcare.

CHAPTER 11

Later Ministry

 N THE previous two chapters, we focused on the Pastors' College and the Stockwell Orphanage as examples of Spurgeon's wider ministry. This is appropriate because, by common consent, these were the two institutions which were closest to his heart. But he was involved in much else besides.

Church planting

It's been estimated that during his lifetime Spurgeon was instrumental in planting a staggering 187 churches. This seems an impossible number, but in Mike Nicholls' book, *C.H. Spurgeon: The Pastor Evangelist,* there is an appendix which carefully lists each individual church.[1] A few of these were actually established fellowships which had fallen on hard times and were on the point of having to close. Spurgeon took a hand in reviving and re-establishing them. But the vast majority of them were new works in pioneering situations, mainly in London and the south-east. Occasionally these plants failed to take root and, somewhere along the line, the church closed. But the vast majority endured and many of these remain lively fellowships to this day. It has been estimated that over half of the English Baptist churches founded between 1865 and 1887 came about thanks to Spurgeon and his students. This was some achievement.

Spurgeon's methods were flexible and varied depending on the context, but often he would work in the following way. To begin with, he would identify an area which seemed like a promising mission opportunity. Then he would send one or two students from the Pastors' College to hold open air preaching services. If some of the local population showed an interest, then he would rent some rooms in the district so that indoor meetings could be held. These rooms might be in a school, a municipal hall, or even attached to a pub – it really didn't matter. If there was further success, with people becoming Christians and a church coming together, then suitable land would be purchased and purpose-built premises erected. Spurgeon had his own lawyer to assist churches in the drawing up of Trust deeds and with any other legal issues which might arise.

The colporteurs

In addition, Spurgeon also established what was known as a 'colportage' society. French in origin, the name colporteur had come to be applied to those who sold Bibles and other Christian literature house to house. Spurgeon established his own society of colporteurs in 1866. There was rapid growth and by 1878 there were ninety-four men engaged in this work. The society held annual conferences at which Spurgeon was the enthusiastic chair. He once invited a certain colporteur on to the platform and asked him to show those gathered how he sold his literature. The man speedily selected a book from his pack and addressed the chair:

> 'Dear Mr Spurgeon, I have a work here that I can highly recommend you to buy. I can speak well of it, for I have read it, and derived great benefit from it. The author is a particular friend of mine, and he is always glad to hear that the colporteurs sell his books, for he knows that they are full of the gospel. The title of the volume is *Trumpet Calls to Christian Energy*, the author is C.H. Spurgeon, and the price is 3s. 6d.; will you buy it?'

To the delight of the audience Spurgeon was more than happy to purchase the book, although we can assume he probably had a copy of it already!

Of course, as with church planting, there were many people involved in this work – it wasn't just Spurgeon. Sometimes Spurgeon is portrayed as an individualist, someone who wasn't really a team player. Certainly he was a big personality and tended to be the leader of anything he was involved in. But he depended greatly on others – his wife, his deacons, his brother, his members of staff, his praying church – in almost everything he did. And, through the institutions and societies he set up, he envisioned, equipped and empowered others for Christian service. Spurgeon may have been unique in the Victorian era. But although he was a one-off, he was not a one-man band. He relied on others and they in turn relied on him.

And much more could still be said about other ministries. Spurgeon helped set up a day school which provided basic education for young children. Evening classes were run at the Tabernacle to help those who were older and who had missed out on such schooling earlier in life. Spurgeon erected seventeen almshouses – houses for the poor – near the Tabernacle. These were all occupied by elderly women. New Park Street had had almshouses from the beginning of the nineteenth century, so this was a continuation of work already started. But Spurgeon developed and expanded this arm of the church's social ministry. For some years he met the women's basic expenses, for example the costs of heating and lighting, from his own pocket. Spurgeon was not just the people's preacher – he was a man who helped ordinary people in practical ways.

Spurgeon at the Tabernacle

But, having said this, we do need to remember that he certainly *was* a preacher, and a quite extraordinary one. The experience of the American visitor to the Tabernacle we read about earlier shows that Spurgeon's popularity as a preacher continued unabated as the nineteenth century wore on. To be sure, his style mellowed a

ABOVE
The colporteur's room

little with age. He moved around the platform less and his delivery became more measured than it had been in his early days. The way he dealt with different Bible verses and themes matured as well. But it was undoubtedly the same gospel, and still the crowds continued to come. Spurgeon was, and remained, the most popular preacher of the Victorian age.

Not only did Spurgeon's style and approach mellow somewhat, but the press comment about him did, too. Gone were the days when his exploits would regularly attract slanderous articles week in, week out. There were still occasional broadsides against him, of course. But, by and large, the hostility had given way to grudging acceptance and, from an increasing number of journalists, real admiration. The uncouth country boy from the Cambridgeshire fens had become one of the established pillars, not only of metropolitan London, but of national life. It wasn't just the lower and middle classes who came to the Tabernacle to hear him. The greatest of Victorian prime ministers, W.E. Gladstone, came one Sunday evening in 1882. There were even rumours (unsubstantiated and almost certainly untrue) that Queen Victoria herself had been to a service incognito! From 1861 and the Tabernacle's opening, to the last time he preached there in 1891, Spurgeon would fill the great auditorium Sunday by Sunday whenever he took the service.

RIGHT
The Spurgeons'
home 'Westwood'

Domestic life

Domestically, things were also positive. In 1869, the Tabernacle deacons built the Spurgeons a new home, 'Hellensburgh House', on the site of their old one in Nightingale Lane. It was a grand building set in spacious grounds. But up until then, the family had been living in an old property which was beset by damp. Few begrudged them this development which was, in any case, paid for by friends and not directly from church funds. As mentioned earlier, in 1880 Charles and Susannah moved from Clapham to South Norwood and to their final, even more comfortable, home, 'Westwood'.

Their marriage continued to be a happy one. Charles wrote Susannah the following lines on an occasion when he was away from home:

> Do not fancy, even for a moment, that absence could make our hearts colder to each other; our attachment is now a perfect union … My sense of your value, and experience of your goodness, are now united to the deep passion of love which was there at the first alone. Every year casts out another anchor to hold me even more firmly to you, though none was needed even from the first. May my own Lord, whose chastening hand has necessitated this absence, give you a secret inward recompense in soul, and also another recompense in the healing of the body! All my heart remains in your keeping.

Charles's continuing and deepening love for his wife was a love which Susannah would always return.

Health problems

However, Charles's letter – especially the references to 'chastening', 'absence' and the need for 'healing of the body' – also indicates that there was sadness, and struggles. The exact nature of Susannah's problem was never spoken of publicly, but in 1869 she had an operation which was performed by Sir James Simpson, a noted gynaecologist. Normally this would have cost over £1,000, but

Sir James, a committed Christian, said he would only send the couple the bill when Charles became Archbishop of Canterbury![2] The Spurgeons believed this operation probably saved Susannah's life, but from this point onwards she was virtually housebound. Certainly she was unable to accompany her husband on any of his many trips and this led to some long absences. All of this was a 'chastening' experience indeed.

To add to this, Charles himself was increasingly unwell. The gout and rheumatism that had seriously afflicted him from at least 1869 steadily worsened. One letter, from 1884, gives a flavour of what he sometimes had to endure:

> I am altogether stranded. I am not able to leave my bed, or to find much rest upon it. The pains of rheumatism, lumbago and sciatica, mingled together, are exceedingly sharp. If I happen to turn a little to the right hand or to the left, I am soon aware that I am dwelling in a body capable of the most acute suffering.

All this, together with continuing kidney problems, served to intensify his tendency to depression and there were times when Spurgeon testified to being brought extremely 'low'. Spurgeon's story is one of faithfulness in the midst of real, and sometimes extreme, suffering.

His physical condition was almost certainly made worse by the cold, damp, smoggy London winters. This was the view of both his doctors and his deacons. They were ready to prescribe what they hoped might be a cure. In the winter that spanned the years 1869–70 Spurgeon had gone on a European tour, the aim of which was to give him rest and improve his health.

Mentone in the south of France … was, he said, 'calculated to make a sick man leap with health'

He returned home significantly better. The final leg of this trip had included a short stay at Mentone (now known as Menton) in the south of France. Spurgeon was extremely taken with this place which was, he said, 'calculated to make a sick man leap with health'. It was suggested he might return there in twelve months' time for a longer stay. In fact, with only one or two exceptions, Spurgeon was to visit Mentone every winter from this point on until his death.

A winter retreat

Mentone was a seaside town on the French Riviera, just a few miles from the border with Italy. With its Mediterranean climate it was usually warm even in winter – a vital requirement for Spurgeon. It was perfect in other ways too. There were comfortable hotels (Spurgeon usually stayed in the Hôtel Beau Rivage), stunning scenery, interesting places to visit and good company. Spurgeon was not an introvert, and being with people he knew and loved helped him recharge his batteries. He nearly always travelled with a small group of friends. Regular companions were his publisher, Joseph Passmore, and his trusted private secretary, J.W. Harrald, who was known as Spurgeon's 'armour bearer' because of the many ways he helped his pastor in the fight of faith.

In addition to these friends, Spurgeon had further stimulating company, for Mentone appears to have been a regular retreat place for a wide variety of well-known Christians. On various trips he met Hudson Taylor (the missionary to China), Archibald McLaren (a well-known Baptist minister from Manchester) and George Muller. All of this was stimulating for Spurgeon. He would often lead weekly communion services in his hotel room. Quite different from the great services at the Tabernacle, these were small, intimate affairs, obviously very moving for those present.

FAR LEFT
Menton today
LEFT
J.W. Harrald

The mention of services shows that, even at Mentone, Spurgeon wasn't always resting. In fact, he wrote numerous letters on various subjects, revised sermons for printing in the *Metropolitan Tabernacle Pulpit*, and gathered material for his books. But life was much more easily paced for him there than in London.

On one occasion, Spurgeon described how he and his party were lying on the beach. He wrote that one of those present was mischievously 'filling our pockets with stones, and rolling Mr Passmore over'. Then, 'who should walk up but Mr McLaren of Manchester, with whom I had a long and pleasant chat. We are to go to Monaco tomorrow together ... Mentone is charming.' All this gives an insight into a side of Spurgeon not normally seen, and also hints at how relaxed he was in Mentone, on the beautiful Côte d'Azur. Spurgeon would habitually spend between a month and six weeks of every winter there. This seems very idyllic, not to say luxurious, for a gospel minister! Few churches would be willing to allow their pastors such generous leave from their duties. But the Tabernacle members could not do enough for Spurgeon, and they recognised the acute and persistent nature of his health problems. Many of his friends were of the opinion that these winter breaks

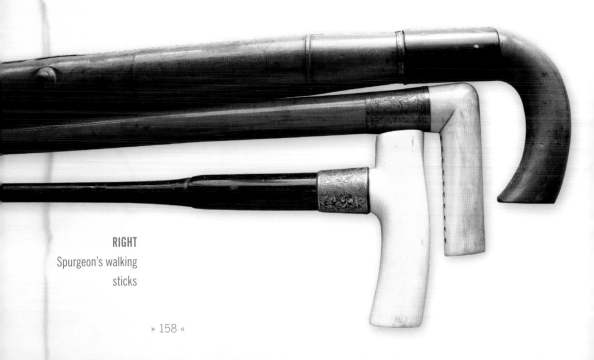

RIGHT
Spurgeon's walking
sticks

prolonged Spurgeon's life. Through the generosity of the Tabernacle church, Spurgeon was spared for further years of fruitful service.

But although Mentone helped, Spurgeon's health continued to be a cause of great concern. In 1879, he was unable to preach at the Tabernacle for a full five months. In 1884, even the sunshine of the French Riviera failed to revive him and he found himself so unwell he was unable to return to London on the date which had been planned. He recovered, but he and others began to recognise that his life was probably entering its final phase.

But there was one last battle to fight before his work on earth was done.

The Downgrade controversy

The Downgrade controversy was so-called because Spurgeon and others believed that central Christian truths were being 'downgraded' in the Church of their day. The main years of the dispute were 1887–88. The course of the controversy was complex and people were not always clear as to what the arguments were about. Fortunately, help is now at hand in the shape of some outstanding research by Mark Hopkins.[3] Working from the available primary sources, Mark has been able to piece together the details of what really happened and isolate the key issues. His book and articles are scholarly but still very readable and, for anyone wanting to understand the controversy in more depth, they are invaluable.

We have already seen that Spurgeon was concerned about an attack on the authority of the Bible from some nineteenth-century scholars (see Chapter 6). Spurgeon used the columns of *The Sword and Trowel* to protest against such liberal theology in both 1887 and 1888. As well as wanting to affirm the entire trustworthiness of the Bible, a particular concern was the importance of the atonement, the word used to describe Christ's death on the cross in our place. This, too, was being downgraded in some quarters. Truths like these, Spurgeon contended, were non-negotiable. Those who rejected them were denying the essentials of the Christian faith. Spurgeon's resignation from the Baptist Union came early in the dispute, in October 1887. He was heavily criticised. Some even thought that his illnesses had unbalanced his mind. But this was most unfair. Spurgeon may have been in pain, but he was quite capable of thinking clearly! Others, many of them friends, noted that he was not at his best in a controversy of this sort. His instinct was to protest and resign rather than to stay and fight for change. The vast majority of his former students, together with the churches Spurgeon had helped establish, chose *not* to resign, either in 1887 or in the years following. Many of these agreed with the main points he was making but thought that resignation was wrong.

Interestingly, Spurgeon did not break fellowship with those who remained in the Baptist Union and were still committed to the same core truths that he was. In November 1887 he wrote to James Culross, a former president of the Union, who profoundly disagreed with Spurgeon's decision to resign:

> Do I need to say that with you ... I have no sort of disagreement, except that you stay in the Union and I am out of it? We shall, according to our light, labour for the same cause. We are all Christians and Baptists, and can find many ways of cooperation.

Nevertheless, Spurgeon's resignation did damage the Union. His son, Thomas, once remarked 'the Baptist Union almost killed my father'. Another minister replied: 'Yes, and your father almost killed the Baptist Union!'

Digging deeper

All of this can obscure the fact that Spurgeon was protesting about real issues. Those who thought that the pastor of the Metropolitan Tabernacle was making something out of nothing were wrong. He was right to say that a number of churches, both inside and outside the Baptist Union, were failing to proclaim the trustworthiness

Some even thought that his illnesses had unbalanced his mind

of Scripture, the truth of the cross or the vital importance of evangelism. Some even doubted that Jesus Christ was fully God as well as fully man. Spurgeon was also absolutely right (I believe) to say that these things *matter*. His decision to resign was one that many close to him regretted. But they did not regret his decision to speak out, and neither should we. Whatever denomination or Church stream we are members of, or whether our church is independent, the issues Spurgeon raised are ones all of us should care about. Perhaps the last word should belong to Susannah Spurgeon. Writing in the *Autobiography*, in the years immediately after her husband's death, she noted:

> I have had abundant proofs that the protest was not in vain. Many, who were far gone in the 'Down-grade', were stopped in their perilous descent, and, by God's grace, were brought back to the Up-line; others, who were unconsciously slipping, were made to stand firmly on the Rock.

Engage

If we are going to be faithful Christians in the twenty-first-century world, we need to be committed to the central truths of the gospel. I've been reminded of this recently, not just through thinking about Spurgeon, but also through reading the 'seven letters to the churches' in Revelation (Revelation chapters 2–3). In these chapters, the different churches are exhorted to various things. These include: persevering through hardships (2:3); excelling in good deeds (3:8); showing love and faith (2:19); and not being 'lukewarm' in Christian living (3:16). All of these challenges are relevant for the modern Church. But these letters also repeatedly urge the rejection of false teaching. Different churches are commended when they do this (eg 2:2) and warned when they do not (eg 2:20).

What is the false teaching we should reject? Or, put positively, what is the truth we should hold on to? Many things could be said, but crucially our focus should always be on Jesus. This is something that Spurgeon reminds us of repeatedly. Jesus is both fully human and fully divine; He died for our sins on the cross; He rose again from the dead and He is coming again to judge both the living and the dead (see John 1:1; Romans 5:6–8; Matthew 28:6; Acts 1:11; 2 Timothy 4:1). Men and women need to come to Him and receive Him as their own personal Saviour and Lord. At different times the Church has failed to be faithful to these absolutely central truths and so has lost the heart of the gospel. Our own age is certainly no different. If we heed this it will be further proof that Spurgeon's stand in the Downgrade was not in vain. Are *we* in danger of downgrading essential Christian truth? If so, we need to hear the call of the Spurgeons to 'stand firmly on the Rock'.

NOTES

1 Some of the information in this and the following paragraph is drawn from Mike Nicholls' *C.H. Spurgeon: The Pastor Evangelist* (Didcot: Baptist Historical Society, 1992) and the chapter which is entitled 'Church Planter', pp.97–114.

2 Here I am relying on information in P.S. Kruppa, *Charles Haddon Spurgeon: A Preacher's Progress* (New York: Garland Publishing, 1982), p.108.

3 M. Hopkins, *Nonconformity's Romantic Generation* (Carlisle: Paternoster Press, 2004), pp.193–248; 'The Down Grade Controversy: New Evidence', *Baptist Quarterly*, Vol 35, No 6 (April 1994), pp.262–278.

CHAPTER 12

'My Work is Done'

O N SUNDAY 7 June 1891, Spurgeon surveyed the huge Tabernacle congregation, took a deep breath, and did what he had done thousands of times before – he began to preach. He was just a few days from his fifty-eighth birthday but he seemed much older – grey-haired, heavy and walking with the aid of a stick. He was recovering from what he described as 'congestion of the lungs' (most likely influenza) and was also suffering from the usual gout. For parts of the service Spurgeon felt so weak he had to hold on to the back of a chair in order to remain standing. On at least one occasion in previous months he had been unable to reach the end of his sermon. But this time he was able to complete his message. His final words were:

> If there is anything that is gracious, generous, kind and tender, lavish and superabundant in love, you always find it in Christ. His service is life, peace, joy. Oh, that you would enter it at once! God help you to enlist under the banner of Jesus Christ!

Those present were clearly moved by the message in general and the conclusion in particular. What would their feelings have been if they had realised this was in fact Spurgeon's last ever sermon at the Tabernacle? This final chapter tells the story of the months leading up to Spurgeon's death, as well as suggesting how best we can remember his truly extraordinary life and ministry.

The last months

On the Friday immediately following his last Tabernacle sermon, Spurgeon, still struggling with the after-effects of flu, was struck down by gout and problems with his kidneys. He was bedridden for three months and often delirious, asking to be taken home although he was, in reality, in his own bedroom. It really seemed as if he might not recover. Press comment was gloomy: 'His life seems to be hanging by a thread' reported one American newspaper.[1] Susannah received letters from Gladstone and a number of Anglican bishops, assuring her of their prayers. But she would have been most comforted by the realisation that thousands at the Tabernacle were praying week after week in special meetings. And, to the surprise of many, Spurgeon's health rallied. By October it was considered possible for him to travel to Mentone. And it was not only Charles who felt strong enough to take the trip. For the first time Susannah was able to accompany her husband to the south of France. The joy of both was unbounded.

The train journey from Herne Hill Station to Dover would have taken them past the Crystal Palace, a place which held so many happy memories for the couple. They and their party would enjoy many happy moments in the three months they would spend in Mentone, too. But Charles would never see the Crystal Palace, or London, again.

Amazingly, he was able to spend some time in Mentone writing. This included revising a little book, *Memories of Stambourne*, for publication. As the title suggests, in it he fondly remembered his childhood growing up with his grandparents in the Stambourne manse. He was still very ill, but for a while appeared to be gaining strength. As late as 16 January 1892 Spurgeon wrote to Joseph Passmore, who this time was not in Mentone with him: 'I have only good news to send you ... I am a shade better.' The Tabernacle church began to look forward to Spurgeon's return home in February.

But, within a week of his letter to Passmore, Spurgeon was struck down once more with what Susannah called the 'gout-mischief' and, even more seriously, acute Bright's disease – the kidney problems with which he had suffered for so long. Sadly, he would have

RIGHT
Memories of Stambourne by C.H. Spurgeon

been in considerable pain, with nausea and vomiting. To Susannah he said: 'Oh Wifey, I have had such a blessed time with my Lord'; to Joseph Harrald, his faithful private secretary and 'armour bearer': 'My work is done.'

By 26 January, he was slipping in and out of consciousness. When death finally came he was in a coma, and mercifully free of pain. With his wife and friends at his bedside, Charles Haddon Spurgeon passed peacefully into the Lord's presence at 11.05pm on Sunday 31 January 1892. A few hours earlier, Harrald had stared out of the window of the hotel and then rushed excitedly to get Susannah, who looked out of the window herself but saw nothing. Harrald was insistent that he had seen a 'company of angels' hovering over the hills, clearly visible against the cloudless blue sky. If this was true (and Harrald was not a man given to flights of fancy) then it was highly appropriate. Spurgeon would not be going home to London, he would be going home to glory. And heaven was ready to welcome him.

The news of Spurgeon's death was met with grief around the world, but no more so than in London, where the Tabernacle congregation were busy constructing a lift so that their pastor would not have to walk up the pulpit steps before preaching. Spurgeon had earlier expressed a desire to be buried in the grounds of the Stockwell Orphanage, but for various reasons this was rejected as unfeasible. Should he then be laid to rest at his beloved Mentone? No, the decision was taken to bring Spurgeon's body back to London, and he was buried in West Norwood cemetery. This was wise as so many in the great city – orphans, pastors, church members – were grieving and wanted to pay their respects. Various memorial services were held in London from Monday 8 February (when the body arrived back in London) to Wednesday 10 February; one was not enough to accommodate all those who wanted to attend. It is estimated that 20,000 people packed the different services on the Wednesday alone. Former students said goodbye to their Guv'nor; orphans said goodbye to their surrogate father; church members said goodbye to their pastor; and countless

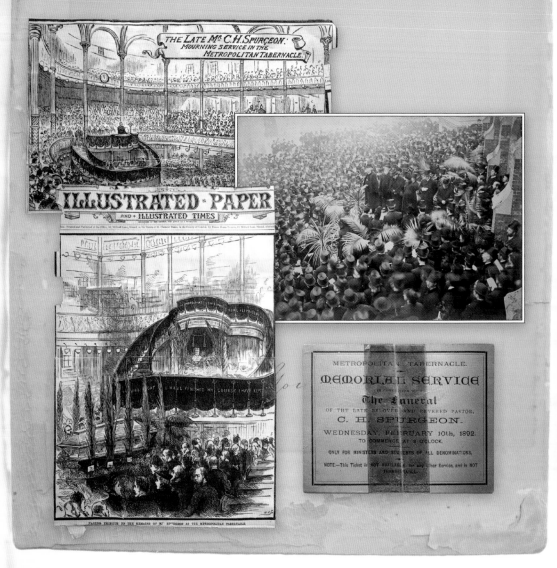

others said goodbye to a man they regarded as perhaps the greatest Christian of the Victorian age.

Finally, on the next day, Thursday 11 February 1892, Spurgeon's body was laid to rest. Eight hundred policemen lined the route from Newington to the cemetery at Norwood. Throughout this final journey, Spurgeon's big pulpit Bible lay open on top of the coffin. The text displayed was none other than Isaiah 45:22, 'Look unto me, and be ye saved, all the ends of the earth ...' (AV) It was a fitting tribute. As in life, so in death, Charles Haddon Spurgeon was urging the world to look to Christ.

ABOVE
Images from Spurgeon's funeral and memorial services

🛈 Digging deeper

The use of the 'Look unto me' text at Spurgeon's funeral suggests the note with which I want to finish this book. Two further quotations will help to drive the point home. The first is from Susannah, reflecting back on the time when her husband used to preach in the Exeter Hall. Sometimes the vast auditorium was too much even for his voice, and one Sunday evening it almost failed. Making one last effort, Spurgeon realised he could only manage a few more audible words. What would he say? Susannah remembered his closing sentences vividly:

> 'Let my name perish, but let Christ's name last for ever! Jesus! *Jesus!* Jesus! Crown Him Lord of all! You will not hear me say anything else. These are my last words in Exeter Hall for this time. Jesus! *Jesus!* Jesus! Crown *Him* Lord of all!'

Having uttered this 'he fell back almost fainting in the chair behind him'. Given all we have seen concerning Spurgeon's life and ministry, we shouldn't be at all surprised that he chose to end his sermon in this way. If Spurgeon only had breath left for one word, then the word he wanted to gasp was 'Jesus'. Spurgeon owed his life to Jesus Christ and responded by spending his life serving his Lord, always depending on His presence and His grace.

The second quotation is from Charles Spurgeon himself. It too comes from the earlier period of his ministry. Spurgeon wrote that coming home from an evening preaching engagement at a London church he saw, in the distance, a tiny light shining out of the gathering gloom as darkness fell. Then there was another, then another, like a trail of stars going up the hill he himself was about to ascend. It was a lamplighter, going up the road, lighting the gas lamps one by one. Spurgeon saw in this a spiritual parable. He said:

> I did not see the lamplighter. I do not know his name, nor his age, nor his residence; but I saw the lights which he had kindled, and

these remained when he himself had gone his way … As I rode along I thought to myself, 'How earnestly do I wish that my life may be spent in lighting one soul after another with the sacred flame of eternal life! I would myself be as much as possible unseen while at my work, and would vanish into eternal brilliance above when my work is done.'

In reality Spurgeon was too big a personality to have remained 'unseen' and he can hardly be said to have vanished, even today! But he did consistently use his extraordinary gifts to point away from himself to Jesus. Thus, throughout his ministry he was able to light one person after another with the 'sacred flame' of eternal life.

◳ Engage

So, how should we remember Spurgeon? We should certainly remember him as the founder of a college, an orphanage and many other evangelistic and charitable works besides. We should remember him as the author of a whole library of wonderful books and as a man deeply committed to the truth of the gospel. And, yes, we should remember Spurgeon as the people's preacher. But most of all we should remember him as someone who, if he only had breath for one word would have gasped 'Jesus', and who lived to light others with that same love and passion. In January 1850 Spurgeon looked to Christ, and from that point on he would spend his whole life looking to his Saviour, and urging others to do the same. We most honour his memory when we follow his example.

NOTE

1 *The Brooklyn Daily Guide*, 17 July 1891. This same reference is used by L. Drummond, *Spurgeon: the Prince of Preachers* (Grand Rapids, Michigan: Kregel, 1992), p. 744.

Acknowledgements

Writing this book has been a wonderful experience for me, made even richer by the help I've received from many people.

A special thank you to colleagues and students at Spurgeon's College for all their encouragement and support in my first year of teaching. Regarding this book specifically, I want to thank our Principal, Nigel Wright, for permission to use all the sources held in our Heritage Room. 'Spurgeon's – for children and young people' have also been extremely helpful, opening up their archives to me and letting me use whatever I found. Thank you to Jean Bowerman, Brett Pitchfork and Keith Hide.

Crawford Telfer from Christian Television Association showed me drafts of the script for the film which accompanies this book and we have been in touch regarding a number of matters since. I hope that, as a 'historical consultant', I've been able to help in some way with the film; certainly contact with CTA has helped me with my writing.

Everyone at CWR has been very encouraging. Sue Wavre and Lynette Brooks read early versions of some of the chapters and were very affirming, as well as offering helpful advice. I am particularly grateful for the faith they have shown in me. Thanks are also due to Patrick Kirwan for his great work with the illustrations and the design. Sheila Jacobs has been a wonderfully thorough and sympathetic editor. Her involvement has been really significant and I'm very much in her debt.

My friend, John Barclay, made some very helpful comments regarding the material on Rothesay in the Introduction. His local knowledge rescued me from a number of errors. My children, Rachel and Joseph, have shown a real interest in what I've been writing. I hope they'll enjoy the end result and be inspired by the example of Spurgeon. My wife, Anne, reads everything I write and her comments on each of the chapters have been very helpful. In this, as in much else, I owe her more than I can say.

All of the people mentioned have greatly improved this book. Any mistakes that remain are, of course, my own responsibility.

C.H. Spurgeon: The People's Preacher is dedicated to my parents, Pam and John, who sacrificed much to give me an education, particularly when I was at university. I deeply appreciate their continued love and support. Written thanks of this kind was certainly overdue.

Peter Morden

Timeline: Charles Haddon Spurgeon

19 June 1834	Birth of Charles Haddon Spurgeon, at Kelvedon, Essex. Parents Eliza (née Jarvis) and John Spurgeon
1835	Goes to live in Stambourne, Essex, with his paternal grandparents, James and Sarah, and his Aunt Ann
1840	Returns to live with his parents, now in Colchester
1844	Richard Knill's prophecy about Spurgeon
17 August 1849	Pupil/teacher at Newmarket school
6 or 13 January 1850	Conversion at Artillery Street Chapel, Colchester
1 February 1850	Writes prayer of consecration in diary
3 May 1850	Baptism in River Lark at Isleham Ferry
17 June 1850	Leaves Newmarket for Cambridge
August 1850	Preaches first sermon, at Teversham, near Cambridge
3 October 1851	First preaches at Waterbeach, Cambridgeshire
18 December 1853	Preaches for first time at New Park Street Chapel, Southwark, London
28 April 1854	Officially pastor of New Park Street
January 1855	*New Park Street Pulpit* first published
February 1855	Preaches for first time at Exeter Hall, the Strand
July 1855	Thomas Medhurst begins training under Spurgeon's supervision: The origins of the Pastors' College (now Spurgeon's College)
8 January 1856	Marriage to Susannah Thompson
20 September 1856	Twin sons, Thomas and Charles, born
19 October 1856	The Surrey Gardens music hall disaster
23 November 1856	Preaches again at the Surrey Gardens music hall
7 October 1857	Preaches to 23,654 people at the Crystal Palace, Sydenham

16 August 1859	Foundation stone laid for Metropolitan Tabernacle
16 March 1861	(Easter, Good Friday) First official service in Metropolitan Tabernacle
1861	Pastors' College moves to basement rooms in the new Tabernacle building
1 January 1865	*The Sword and Trowel* magazine begins publication
1866	The Colportage Society (for distribution and sale of Christian literature) formed
6 January 1868	His brother, James Archer Spurgeon, becomes assistant pastor at the Metropolitan Tabernacle
1868	Almshouses built
9 September 1869	Stockwell Orphanage for boys is officially opened
1871	First visits Mentone, South of France
1874	Pastors' College moves to purpose-built premises in Temple Street, south London
1875	Susannah Spurgeon begins book fund for pastors; Thomas Johnson begins study at the Pastors' College
28 July 1878	Preaches at Rothesay, on the Isle of Bute, in the Firth of Clyde, Scotland, to as many as 20,000 people
1879	Girl's wing of orphanage opened
January 1880	Death of Anne Hillyard, original benefactor of Stockwell Orphanage
1880	Move from Nightingale Lane, Clapham, to 'Westwood', Upper Norwood
8 January 1882	Gladstone attends a Sunday evening service at the Metropolitan Tabernacle
August 1887	Writes his first Downgrade article in *The Sword and Trowel*
28 October 1887	Resigns from the Baptist Union
7 June 1891	Last sermon in Metropolitan Tabernacle
31 January 1892	Death in Mentone, South of France
11 February 1892	Burial in West Norwood cemetery

Day and Residential Courses
Counselling Training
Leadership Development
Biblical Study Courses
Regional Seminars
Ministry to Women
Daily Devotionals
Books and Videos
Conference Centre

Trusted all Over the World

CWR HAS GAINED A WORLDWIDE reputation as a centre of excellence for Bible-based training and resources. From our headquarters at Waverley Abbey House, Farnham, England, we have been serving God's people for over 40 years with a vision to help apply God's Word to everyday life and relationships. The daily devotional *Every Day with Jesus* is read by nearly a million readers an issue in more than 150 countries, and our unique courses in biblical studies and pastoral care are respected all over the world. Waverley Abbey House provides a conference centre in a tranquil setting.

For free brochures on our seminars and courses, conference facilities, or a catalogue of CWR resources, please contact us at the following address.
CWR, Waverley Abbey House, Waverley Lane, Farnham, Surrey GU9 8EP, UK

Telephone: **+44 (0)1252 784700**
Email: **mail@cwr.org.uk**
Website: **www.cwr.org.uk**

Spurgeon brought to life

This riveting drama documentary goes beyond the text of the book to follow the trials and triumphs of C.H. Spurgeon with vivid historical accuracy.

   This powerful, inspirational film convincingly brings the 'people's preacher' to life, showing him to be a man whose eventful - and sometimes controversial - life is relevant to the twenty-first century.

   Made by the award winning producers, Christian Television Association (www.cta.uk.com), and filmed on location in England, Scotland, France and Germany, the film faithfully recreates the times and captures the spirit and message of a man mightily used by God.

Approximately 75 minutes, colour, region-free PAL DVD
EAN: 5027957001220

£15.99 inc VAT

THE PEOPLE'S PREACHER
C. H. Spurgeon

DRAMA DOCUMENTARY
A CTA Production

Price correct at time of printing.